TARGET YOUR MATHS

Year 4

Stephen Pearce

Elmwood Education

First published 2014 by
Elmwood Education
Unit 5 Mallow Park
Watchmead
Welwyn Garden City
Herts. AL7 1GX
Tel. 01707 333232

ISBN 9781 906 622 282

Numerical answers are published in a separate book.

Typeset and illustrated by Tech-Set Ltd., Gateshead, Tyne and Wear.

PREFACE

Target your Maths has been written for pupils in Year 4 and their teachers.

The intention of the book is to provide teachers with material to teach the statutory requirements set out in the Year 4 Programme of Study for Mathematics in the renewed 2014 National Curriculum Framework

In the renewed Framework the Year 4 Programme of Study has been organised into eight domains or sub-domains.

Number – number and place value
Number – addition and subtraction
Number – multiplication and division
Number – fractions (including decimals)
Measurement
Geometry – properties of shape
Geometry – position and direction
Statistics

The structure of **Target your Maths 4** corresponds to that of the Year 4 Programme of Study. There is also a Review section at the end of the book.

All the statutory requirements of the Year 4 Programme of Study are covered in **Target your Maths 4**. Appendix I of the Teacher's Answer Book matches the statutory requirements and some essential non-statutory guidance with the relevant pages in this book. Most requirements are covered by more than one page. The author believes it is important that teachers have ample material from which to select.

Each single or double page lesson in this book is divided into four sections:

Introduction: the learning intention expressed as a target and, where necessary, clearly worked examples.

Section A: activities based upon work previously covered. This generally matches the requirements for Year 3 pupils. This section can be used to remind children of work previously covered, as well as providing material for the less confident child.

Section B: activities based upon the requirements for Year 4 pupils. Most children should be able to work successfully at this level.

Section C: activities providing extension material for the faster workers and for those who need to be moved quickly onto more challenging tasks. The work in this section generally matches the requirements for Year 5 pupils. Problems in Section C can also provide useful material for discussion in the plenary session.

The correspondence of the three sections A–C to the requirements for different year groups provides a simple, manageable structure for planning differentiated activities and for both the formal and informal assessment of children's progress. The commonality of the content pitched at different levels also allows for progression within the lesson. Children acquiring confidence at one level find they can successfully complete activities at the next level.

There is, of course, no set path through either the Year 4 Programme of Study or **Target your Maths 4** but teachers may find Appendices II and III in the Teacher's Answer Book useful for planning purposes. In these tables one possible approach is given to the planning of the curriculum throughout the year.

In Appendix II the **Target your Maths** pages for each domain are organised into a three term school year. In Appendix III the work for each term is arranged into twelve blocks, each approximately corresponding to one week's work. For the sake of simplicity blocks are generally based upon one domain only.

The structure as set out in Appendices II and III enables teachers to develop concepts progressively throughout the year and provides pupils with frequent opportunities to consolidate previous learning.

The author is indebted to many colleagues who have assisted him in this work. He is particularly grateful to Sharon Granville and Davina Tunkel for their invaluable advice and assistance.

Stephen Pearce

CONTENTS

TARGET To use an understanding of place value to read and write numbers beyond 1000.

The value of a digit and the way we read it depends upon its place in the number.

Example

Th	H	T	U
4	5	2	7

The 4 has a value of 4000.
The 5 has a value of 500.
The 2 has a value of 20.
The 7 has a value of 7.

4527 reads as:
four thousand five hundred and twenty-seven.

TAKE CARE when a number has zeros in it.
9300 is read as nine thousand three hundred.
9030 is read as nine thousand and thirty.
9003 is read as nine thousand and three.

 A

1 Copy the table, writing each distance in figures.

Place	Round distance to Land's End (miles)
London	two hundred and ninety-seven
Glasgow	five hundred and seventy-three
Blackpool	four hundred and five
Plymouth	eighty-nine
Bristol	two hundred
Aberdeen	six hundred and ninety-two
Shrewsbury	three hundred and three
John o'Groats	eight hundred and sixty-eight

2 These figures also show the road distance between Land's End and other places in Great Britain. Write each distance in words.

a)	Birmingham	281 miles	g)	Dundee	642 miles
b)	Newcastle	498 miles	h)	Bournemouth	206 miles
c)	Leicester	320 miles	i)	Exeter	123 miles
d)	Edinburgh	574 miles	j)	Inverness	740 miles
e)	Leeds	407 miles	k)	Manchester	361 miles
f)	Aberystwyth	313 miles	l)	Portsmouth	259 miles

B

1 Copy the table, writing each distance in figures.

Route	Air Distance (miles)
Montreal – Anchorage	three thousand one hundred
Amsterdam – Cairo	two thousand and forty-two
Tokyo – Delhi	one thousand eight hundred and six
Lagos – Beijing	eight thousand and thirty
Chicago – Sydney	nine thousand three hundred and twenty-four
Santiago – Nairobi	seven thousand five hundred and forty-seven
Johannesburg – Rome	four thousand eight hundred and one
Washington – Buenos Aires	six thousand and ninety seven

2 These figures show the air distance between London and other cities. Write each distance in words.

a)	Moscow	1550 miles	f)	Perth	9248 miles
b)	Buenos Aires	6985 miles	g)	Honolulu	7254 miles
c)	Mexico City	5703 miles	h)	Paris	220 miles
d)	Delhi	4169 miles	i)	Washington	3672 miles
e)	Rome	898 miles	j)	Sydney	10 565 miles

C

Write the size of the crowd at each football stadium in words.

1	Arsenal	60 000	**6**	Manchester United	75 837
2	Sunderland	39 095	**7**	Blackpool	15 309
3	Liverpool	44 171	**8**	Tottenham Hotspur	36 064
4	Celtic	50 904	**9**	Newcastle	49 540
5	Stoke	27 228	**10**	Wembley	80 612

Copy each sentence writing the number in figures.

11 Three hundred thousand people live in Coventry.

12 The house was sold for a quarter of a million pounds.

13 Shayla won six hundred and ninety thousand pounds on the Lottery.

14 The film was seen by half a million people in one week.

15 One hundred and eight thousand cars used the ferry last year.

e place value of each digit in a four-digit

s place in the number.

PARTITIONING

ue of 3000.
ue of 800.
ue of 40.
ue of 6.

Knowing the value of each digit means that you are able to partition the number.

$3846 = 3000 + 800 + 40 + 6$

A

Copy and complete.

1. $186 = 100 + 80 + \square$
2. $732 = 700 + \square + 2$
3. $519 = \square + 10 + 9$
4. $248 = 200 + \square + 8$

5. $983 = \square + 80 + 3$
6. $427 = 400 + 20 + \square$
7. $651 = 600 + \square + 1$
8. $374 = \square + 70 + 4$

Write down the value of the digit underlined.

9. 5<u>2</u>6
10. <u>3</u>98
11. 84<u>5</u>
12. 1<u>6</u>3
13. 27<u>8</u>
14. <u>6</u>14
15. 9<u>5</u>7
16. <u>4</u>32
17. 70<u>9</u>
18. 3<u>8</u>1

Add 100 to:

19. 374
20. 519
21. 206
22. 843
23. 487
24. 240
25. 652
26. 318
27. 975
28. 731

B

What is the value of the digit underlined?

1. 5<u>4</u>6
2. <u>2</u>09
3. 734<u>8</u>
4. <u>1</u>627
5. 975<u>2</u>
6. 31<u>8</u>9
7. <u>8</u>503
8. 4<u>2</u>16

Partition these numbers as in the example.

9. 3597
10. 6241
11. 1705
12. 8369
13. 4623
14. 7158
15. 2836
16. 9418

What needs to be added or subtracted to change:

17. 647 to 687
18. 4539 to 2539
19. 1821 to 1521
20. 2703 to 7703
21. 4159 to 4859
22. 6204 to 6264
23. 3837 to 7837
24. 8916 to 8416
25. 4575 to 1575
26. 2823 to 2893?

C

Take 40 from:

1. 1265
2. 4897
3. 536
4. 2971
5. 8104

Add 500 to:

6. 3290
7. 847
8. 27 523
9. 61
10. 4

Take 300 from:

11. 5924
12. 32 181
13. 7763
14. 11 358
15. 49 096

Add 6000 to:

16. 8020
17. 17
18. 25 863
19. 409
20. 39 116

What needs to be added or subtracted to change:

21. 24 173 to 31 173
22. 5908 to 5858
23. 3090 to 1000
24. 9998 to 100 000?

Copy and complete.

25. $3472 = \square + 72$
26. $51\,068 = \square + 68$
27. $2259 = 2009 + \square$
28. $64\,387 = 60\,007 + \square$

TARGET   To order and compare numbers beyond 1000.

Example
Put these numbers in order with the smallest first.
8724, 7824, 8472

Look at the thousands first.
If the thousands are the same
look at the hundreds.

The correct order is 7824, 8472, 8724.

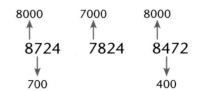

8000	7000	8000
↑	↑	↑
8724	7824	8472
↓		↓
700		400

A

Which number is smaller?

1. 75 or 57
2. 23 or 32
3. 891 or 918
4. 604 or 408
5. 768 or 687

Which number is larger?

6. 673 or 736
7. 845 or 584
8. 120 or 201
9. 329 or 293
10. 782 or 827

Place these sets of numbers in order starting with the smallest.

11. 251   125   152   215
12. 693   936   639   963
13. 847   784   874   748
14. 324   432   423   342

Answer True or False

15. 38 < 83
16. 907 > 970
17. 8 × 4 < 9 × 3
18. 60 ÷ 2 > 6 × 5

B

Copy and put < or > in the box.

1. 5318 ☐ 5138
2. 1479 ☐ 1749
3. 7204 ☐ 7402
4. 4635 ☐ 4536
5. 6989 ☐ 6899
6. 2415 ☐ 2514
7. 8738 ☐ 8387
8. 3989 ☐ 4001

Put these numbers in order starting with the smallest.

9. 3974   4397   3794   4379
10. 5628   5826   6258   5682
11. 9318   8913   8931   9183
12. 2202   2002   2020   2220

What needs to be added or subtracted to change:

13. 2935 to 2635
14. 4718 to 4788
15. 6307 to 8307
16. 1925 to 1975
17. 9449 to 5449
18. 7803 to 7863

C

Work out the number that is halfway between these numbers.

1. 2270 ←☐→ 2370
2. 1880 ←☐→ 1940
3. 13 400 ←☐→ 14 400
4. 1500 ←☐→ 2000
5. 5700 ←☐→ 6100
6. 8970 ←☐→ 9030
7. 24 400 ←☐→ 25 000
8. 3100 ←☐→ 4000

What needs to be added or subtracted to change:

9. 6871 to 6661
10. 3500 to 3924
11. 4710 to 5000
12. 2587 to 3687?

13. Use these digits once each.

Make two 3-digit numbers which give:
a) the largest possible total
b) the smallest possible total
c) the largest possible difference
d) the smallest possible difference.

TARGET To count on in multiples of any single-digit number.

Example
Start at 54.
Count on five 6s.

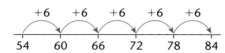

```
      +6   +6   +6   +6   +6
     54   60   66   72   78   84
```

A

Start at 0.
What number do you reach if you count on:

1. seven steps of 5

2. nine steps of 2

3. six steps of 3

4. eight steps of 4

5. twelve steps of 10

6. four steps of 8

7. fourteen steps of 2

8. seventeen steps of 10

9. eleven steps of 3

10. twelve steps of 5

11. seven steps of 8

12. twelve steps of 4

13. thirteen steps of 3

14. eleven steps of 10

15. nine steps of 8

16. seventeen steps of 2

17. eleven steps of 4

18. fifteen steps of 5?

B

What number do you reach?

1. Start at 16.
   Count on six 2s.

2. Start at 44.
   Count on five 4s.

3. Start at 65.
   Count on seven 5s.

4. Start at 21.
   Count on four 7s.

5. Start at 21.
   Count on eight 3s.

6. Start at 870.
   Count on six 10s.

7. Start at 72.
   Count on four 8s.

8. Start at 24.
   Count on six 6s.

9. Start at 5988.
   Count on nine 2s.

10. Start at 54.
    Count on five 9s.

11. Start at 68.
    Count on eight 4s.

12. Start at 3275.
    Count on six 5s.

C

What number do you reach?

1. Start at 263.
   Count on seven 10s.

2. Start at 14 792.
   Count on eleven 5s.

3. Start at 9130.
   Count on five 1000s.

4. Start at 3750.
   Count on five 25s.

5. Start at 533 610.
   Count on six 100s.

6. Start at 6230.
   Count on eight 50s.

7. Start at 30 782.
   Count on twelve 10s.

8. Start at 248.
   Count on nine 5s.

9. Start at 64.
   Count on seven 1000s.

10. Start at 810.
    Count on six 25s.

11. Start at 9406.
    Count on nine 100s.

12. Start at 61 723.
    Count on seven 50s.

TARGET   To count on in multiples of 10, 25, 50, 100 and 1000.

Example
Start at 4236.
Count on five 50s.

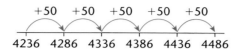

+50   +50   +50   +50   +50
4236 4286 4336 4386 4436 4486

A

Start at 0.
What number do you
reach if you count on:

1 six 5s

2 seven 10s

3 four 50s

4 five 100s

5 nine 5s

6 six 10s

7 five 50s

8 seven 100s?

Write the first six numbers
in each sequence.

9 Start at 27.
   Count on in 10s.

10 Start at 30.
    Count on in 50s.

11 Start at 63.
    Count on in 100s.

12 Start at 6.
    Count on in 5s.

13 Start at 4.
    Count on in 10s.

14 Start at 120.
    Count on in 50s.

15 Start at 9.
    Count on in 100s.

16 Start at 23.
    Count on in 5s.

B

Count on in 10s.

1 80 from 1250

2 60 from 580

3 50 from 3179

4 90 from 6943

Count on in 50s.

5 six 50s from 510

6 nine 50s from 2650

7 five 50s from 1895

8 eight 50s from 9381

Count on in 100s.

9 400 from 5340

10 700 from 574

11 600 from 7058

12 900 from 3699

Count on in 25s.

13 five 25s from 60

14 four 25s from 8435

15 six 25s from 272

16 seven 25s from 846

Count on in 1000s.

17 3000 from 285

18 5000 from 67

19 4000 from 8

20 6000 from 2139

C

What number do you reach if
you count on:

1 five 100s from 25 738

2 four 1000s from 6204

3 three 10 000s from 21 960

4 eight 100s from 10 805

5 six 1000s from 79 320

6 five 10 000s from 175 000

7 seven 100s from 369 429

8 five 1000s from 107 517

9 nine 10 000s from 53 701?

Continue each sequence.

10 Start at 9661.
    Count on eight 50s.

11 Start at 454 638.
    Count on seven 25s.

12 Start at 292 086.
    Count on four 10 000s.

13 Start at 166 207.
    Count on nine 500s.

14 Start at 8040.
    Count on eight 250s.

15 Start at 861 135.
    Count on six 10 000s.

16 Start at 175 204.
    Count on seven 5000s.

17 Start at 419 136.
    Count on five 2500s.

TARGET   To find 10, 100 and 1000 more or less than any given number.

Examples

1875 + 10 = 1885   3432 + 100 = 3532   59 + 1000 = 1059
5294 − 10 = 5284   2067 − 100 = 1967   6485 − 1000 = 5485

A

Work out

1. 320 + 10
2. 672 + 10
3. 243 + 10
4. 986 + 10

5. 537 − 10
6. 754 − 10
7. 125 − 10
8. 890 − 10

9. 471 + 100
10. 650 + 100
11. 120 + 100
12. 704 + 100

13. 530 − 100
14. 380 − 100
15. 844 − 100
16. 267 − 100

17. Sian's bottle of medicine holds 135 ml. She takes two 10 ml doses. How much medicine is left?

18. Howard drives 100 miles. He still has 152 miles to go. How long is his journey?

B

Work out

1. 1632 + 10
2. 2308 + 10
3. 8257 − 10
4. 4509 − 10

5. 3746 + 100
6. 6983 + 100
7. 9070 − 100
8. 5465 − 100

9. 8321 + 1000
10. 2947 + 1000
11. 3596 + 1000
12. 7045 + 1000

13. 1178 − 1000
14. 5633 − 1000
15. 9062 − 1000
16. 4919 − 1000

17. Marcia earns £2938 each month. In April her monthly pay goes up by £1000. How much does she now earn?

18. A concert hall has seats for 1068 people. Two blocks of 100 seats are reserved. How many seats are on sale to the public?

C

Work out

1. 28 919 + 10
2. 13 168 + 10
3. 150 000 − 10
4. 234 846 − 10
5. 32 475 + 100
6. 15 924 + 100
7. 167 353 − 100
8. 421 050 − 100
9. 74 298 + 1000
10. 35 873 + 1000
11. 199 402 + 1000
12. 590 957 + 1000
13. 59 749 − 1000
14. 23 004 − 1000
15. 170 491 − 1000
16. 942 816 − 1000

17. A crowd of 50 017 watch a football match. 100 of the spectators are guests of the home team club. How many of the crowd are paying spectators?

18. A return flight between London and Perth travels a total distance of 18 492 miles. A change of airport in the UK adds 10 miles to each journey. How long is the return flight now?

TARGET   To count backwards through zero.

Negative numbers (below zero) | Positive numbers (above zero)

−10 −9 −8 −7 −6 −5 −4 −3 −2 −1 0 1 2 3 4 5 6 7 8 9 10

A

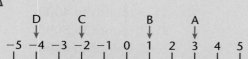

1 What number is shown by each of the letters A–D?

Count back:

2 3 from A   **4** 5 from A

3 4 from B   **5** 2 from B.

What number do you reach?

6 Start at 0.   **10** Start at 1.
Count back 4.   Count back 5.

7 Start at 5.   **11** Start at 3.
Count back 6.   Count back 4.

8 Start at 2.   **12** Start at 4.
Count back 5.   Count back 7.

9 Start at 4.   **13** Start at 2.
Count back 6.   Count back 6.

B

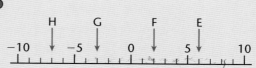

1 What number is shown by each of the letters E–H?

Count back:

2 7 from F   **4** 10 from F

3 5 from E   **5** 8 from E.

What number do you reach?

6 Start at 4.   **10** Start at 0.
Count back 8.   Count back 6.

7 Start at 1.   **11** Start at 8.
Count back 9.   Count back 11.

8 Start at 9.   **12** Start at 3.
Count back 12.   Count back 8.

9 Start at 5.   **13** Start at 7.
Count back 10.   Count back 9.

C

Copy and complete.

1 4 2 0 −2 ☐ ☐ ☐

2 16 12 8 4 ☐ ☐ ☐

3 15 12 9 6 ☐ ☐ ☐

4 2 1 ☐ ☐ ☐ −3 −4

5 3 1 ☐ ☐ ☐ −7 −9

6 10 5 ☐ ☐ ☐ −15 −20

What number do you reach?

7 Start at −3. Count on 7.

8 Start at −1. Count on 8.

9 Start at −8. Count on 6.

10 Start at −6. Count on 11.

11 Start at −10. Count on 9.

12 Start at −5. Count on 15.

TARGET   To round any number to the nearest 10, 100 or 1000.

TO THE NEAREST 10
Look at the units.
5 or more, round up.
Less than 5, round down.

Examples
29 rounds to 30
153 rounds to 150
2645 rounds to 2650

TO THE NEAREST 100
Look at the 10s and units.
50 or more, round up.
Less than 50, round down.

529 rounds to 500
8153 rounds to 8200
2645 rounds to 2600

TO THE NEAREST 1000
Look at the 100s and 10s.
500 or more, round up.
Less than 500, round down.

3529 rounds to 4000
8153 rounds to 8000
2645 rounds to 3000

A

Copy and complete by rounding to the nearest 10.

1. 42 rounds to ☐
2. 26 rounds to ☐
3. 88 rounds to ☐
4. 13 rounds to ☐
5. 65 rounds to ☐
6. 71 rounds to ☐
7. 37 rounds to ☐
8. 54 rounds to ☐

Round to the nearest 100.

9. 930 rounds to ☐
10. 290 rounds to ☐
11. 720 rounds to ☐
12. 680 rounds to ☐
13. 450 rounds to ☐
14. 340 rounds to ☐
15. 210 rounds to ☐
16. 860 rounds to ☐

B

Round to the nearest 10.

1. 258
2. 763
3. 535
4. 481
5. 1674
6. 5727
7. 2099
8. 8332

Round to the nearest 100.

9. 1341
10. 764
11. 2948
12. 6572
13. 257
14. 3925
15. 7383
16. 4536

Round to the nearest:
a) 10   b) 100   c) 1000.

17. 5248
18. 972
19. 2494
20. 3627
21. 8316
22. 1753
23. 9560
24. 4838

25. 7183
26. 3929
27. 1515
28. 6072
29. 2692
30. 9147
31. 236
32. 8551

C

Round to the nearest 100.

1. 58 393
2. 19 625
3. 34 826
4. 79 454
5. 81 528
6. 25 260
7. 19 182
8. 43 739

Round to the nearest 1000.

9. 15 938
10. 12 273
11. 56 717
12. 94 354
13. 34 469
14. 29 540
15. 61 177
16. 25 635

Approximate by rounding to the nearest 10.

17. 31 + 68
18. 47 + 29
19. 55 + 34
20. 81 − 44
21. 72 − 48
22. 96 − 29

Approximate by rounding the first number.

23. 32 × 2
24. 59 × 4
25. 18 × 8
26. 67 × 3
27. 43 × 5
28. 51 × 6

TARGET   To round any number to the nearest 10, 100 or 1000.

Always look at the column to the right of that to which you are rounding.
If the number in that column is: 5 or more, round up
less than 5, round down

Examples

TO THE NEAREST 10
8438 rounds to 8440
6571 rounds to 6570
 925 rounds to 930

TO THE NEAREST 100
8438 rounds to 8400
6571 rounds to 6600
 925 rounds to 900

TO THE NEAREST 1000
8438 rounds to 8000
6571 rounds to 7000
 925 rounds to 1000

A

Round to the nearest 10.

1 67
2 31
3 45
4 79
5 24
6 52
7 18
8 86
9 63
10 95

Round to the nearest 100.

11 320
12 471
13 948
14 854
15 283
16 590
17 819
18 253
19 160
20 737

Round to the nearest pound.

21 £6·50
22 £8·80
23 £5·10
24 £4·60
25 £2·30
26 £9·20
27 £5·90
28 £2·70
29 £7·40
30 £3·50

B

Round to the nearest 10.

1 136
2 841
3 529
4 263
5 915
6 2692
7 4357
8 1034
9 3715
10 8478

Round to the nearest 100.

11 4728
12 253
13 2561
14 837
15 1484
16 5205
17 3193
18 2946
19 9371
20 6652

Round to the nearest:
a) 10   b) 100   c) 1000.

21 1284
22 881
23 5929
24 8754
25 3275
26 6592
27 9415
28 4163
29 2607
30 7358

C

Round to the nearest 10.

1 11 344
2 42 717
3 35 285
4 73 162
5 121 559
6 53 450
7 117 076
8 22 923
9 234 395
10 390 831

Round to the nearest 100.

11 24 183
12 50 815
13 172 262
14 16 747
15 298 354
16 502 526
17 47 391
18 631 653
19 180 438
20 363 972

Round to the nearest:
a) 10   b) 100   c) 1000.

21 62 361
22 118 097
23 49 505
24 30 153
25 291 838
26 27 014
27 104 286
28 53 472
29 215 625
30 170 059

TARGET To read Roman numerals to 100.

The Ancient Romans used letters to stand for numbers. Roman numerals were used in Europe until they were replaced by the Arabic numbers we use today. However, Roman numerals are still used for some things, such as the names of kings and queens or on some clock faces.

Letters	Values
I	1
V	5
X	10
L	50
C	100
D	500
M	1000

Rules For Forming Numbers

1 Repeated letters are added. V, L and D are never repeated. Only repeat a letter three times.
Example   XXX = 10 + 10 + 10 = 30

2 Larger value first means add.
Example   XXVII = 10 + 10 + 5 + 1 + 1 = 27

3 Smaller value first means subtract.
Examples   IV = 5 − 1 = 4   IX = 10 − 1 = 9

a) Only subtract one number from another.
Example   8 is VIII not IIX

b) Only subtract I, X and C, not V, L or D.
Example   45 is XLV not VL

c) Only subtract the nearest value out of I, X and C.
Example   99 is XCIX not IC

A

Write as Arabic numbers.

1 IV
2 XVIII
3 XXII
4 XXXV
5 XI
6 VII
7 XX
8 XXXIX
9 V
10 XXIV
11 XIII
12 XXXI
13 XXVII
14 XL
15 XIX
16 XXV

Write as Roman numerals.

17 3
18 26
19 30
20 11
21 37
22 15
23 9
24 34
25 23
26 10
27 17
28 32
29 29
30 14
31 38

Copy the sentences changing the numbers to Roman numerals.

32 George 6 was the father of Elizabeth 2 and the brother of Edward 8.

33 At midnight both hands of the clock pointed to 12.

34 In 2000 the Games of the 27 Olympiad were held in Sydney.

35 Benedict 16 became Pope in 2005.

B

Write as Arabic numbers.

1. XLII
2. LXXIX
3. XCVI
4. LIV
5. XLIX
6. LXXXI
7. XCIII
8. LX
9. LXXV
10. LVIII
11. XCIX
12. XLV
13. LXXXIV
14. LXVI
15. XC
16. XLIX

Write as Roman numerals.

17. 94
18. 48
19. 63
20. 89
21. 95
22. 74
23. 41
24. 59
25. 92
26. 83
27. 46
28. 68
29. 97
30. 55
31. 44

Copy each sentence changing the numbers to Roman numerals.

32. The first Roman Emperor, Augustus Caesar, died in AD 14 aged 75.

33. The conquest of Britain began in AD 43.

34. Boudicca's revolt against Roman rule was crushed in AD 61.

35. The centurion commanded 80 soldiers but only 59 survived the battle.

C

Write as Arabic numbers.

1. CXXXVI
2. DCXIV
3. CCXCV
4. DCCCXXIX
5. CCCXLII
6. DCCXXXIV
7. CMIII
8. CDLXXX
9. DLIII
10. DCCCXCVIII
11. CMLXVII
12. DCCXL
13. CLXXI
14. CCVIII
15. CDXXII
16. DCLXIX

Write as Roman numerals.

17. 443
18. 580
19. 109
20. 985
21. 212
22. 678
23. 724
24. 352
25. 849
26. 496
27. 928
28. 164
29. 791
30. 536
31. 652

Write the distance between each pair of Roman cities in Roman numerals.

32. Norwich – Leicester   119 miles
33. Dorchester – Lincoln   246 miles
34. London – Carlisle   314 miles
35. Dover – Bath   187 miles
36. York – Exeter   298 miles

Write the distance to Rome from each city in Arabic numbers.

37. Nice   CDXXXIII miles
38. Bari   CCLXXIX miles
39. Geneva   DLIV miles
40. Paris   DCCCLXXXVI miles
41. Florence   CLXXII miles

TARGET To use addition and subtraction facts to +/− multiples of 10 and 100 mentally.

A

Work out

1. 8 + 7
2. 9 + 6
3. 7 + 5
4. 5 + 8

5. 6 + 8
6. 9 + 7
7. 8 + 4
8. 7 + 9

9. 4 + 7
10. 9 + 5
11. 7 + 6
12. 8 + 9

13. 5 + 7
14. 8 + 6
15. 9 + 9
16. 7 + 8

17. 14 − 6
18. 16 − 9
19. 13 − 4
20. 20 − 14

21. 15 − 7
22. 18 − 9
23. 12 − 5
24. 14 − 9

25. 20 − 8
26. 11 − 4
27. 15 − 6
28. 17 − 8

29. 13 − 7
30. 16 − 8
31. 20 − 13
32. 19 − 5

Copy and complete.
Use the three given numbers only.

33. 25 + 18 = 43

☐ + ☐ = ☐
43 − ☐ = ☐
☐ − ☐ = ☐

34. 37 + 29 = 66

☐ + ☐ = ☐
☐ − ☐ = 37
☐ − ☐ = ☐

B

Work out

1. 90 + 40
2. 50 + 90
3. 80 + 50
4. 60 + 90

5. 70 + 70
6. 150 − 80
7. 170 − 90
8. 140 − 70

9. 160 − 50
10. 130 − 70
11. 700 + 800
12. 900 + 300

13. 600 + 700
14. 800 + 800
15. 1100 + 900
16. 1500 − 700

17. 1200 − 600
18. 1400 − 800
19. 1600 − 900
20. 1900 − 700

For each fact below write three related facts.

21. 36 + 19 = 55
22. 83 − 54 = 29
23. 48 + 24 = 72
24. 61 − 27 = 34

C

Copy and complete.

1. 80 + ☐ = 120
2. 50 + ☐ = 110
3. 60 + ☐ = 130
4. 90 + ☐ = 150

5. 70 + ☐ = 140
6. 110 − ☐ = 30
7. 130 − ☐ = 90
8. 170 − ☐ = 80

9. 200 − ☐ = 40
10. 140 − ☐ = 50
11. 700 + ☐ = 1600
12. 4000 + ☐ = 12 000

13. 800 + ☐ = 1700
14. 6000 + ☐ = 11 000
15. 900 + ☐ = 1300
16. 1200 − ☐ = 300

17. 16 000 − ☐ = 8000
18. 2000 − ☐ = 1100
19. 15 000 − ☐ = 7000
20. 1300 − ☐ = 600

For each set of numbers write four related + and − facts.

21. 500, 220, 280
22. 88, 134, 46
23. 330, 470, 800
24. 135, 247, 112

TARGET To use addition and subtraction facts to find other related facts.

A

Write the answers only.

1. 5 + 9
2. 8 + 5
3. 6 + 7
4. 4 + 8

5. 7 + 7
6. 9 + 6
7. 6 + 8
8. 8 + 9

9. 14 − 8
10. 16 − 9
11. 12 − 7
12. 15 − 6

13. 13 − 7
14. 17 − 8
15. 15 − 7
16. 18 − 9

17. Use the given fact to work out the other facts.

$$12 - \square = 9$$
$$13 - \square = 9$$
$$14 - \square = 9$$
$$15 - 6 = 9$$

$$16 - \square = 9$$
$$17 - \square = 9$$
$$18 - \square = 9$$
$$19 - \square = 9$$

B

Write the answers only.

1. 40 + 70
2. 90 + 50
3. 70 + 60
4. 30 + 90

5. 60 + 90
6. 80 + 60
7. 50 + 70
8. 90 + 80

9. 120 − 60
10. 140 − 70
11. 170 − 90
12. 150 − 80

13. 130 − 40
14. 160 − 80
15. 180 − 70
16. 140 − 50

17. 700 + 900
18. 800 + 400
19. 500 + 800
20. 600 + 500

21. 800 + 700
22. 900 + 900
23. 700 + 500
24. 600 + 700

25. 1500 − 900
26. 1200 − 800
27. 1800 − 900
28. 1400 − 600

29. 1300 − 800
30. 1700 − 800
31. 1500 − 600
32. 1600 − 900

$$14 - 8 = 6$$

Use the above fact to make other related facts with an answer of:

33. 8
34. 60
35. 1400
36. 6000
37. 140
38. 800

39. Find five pairs of 3-digit numbers that total 1000. You cannot use multiples of 100.

C

Copy and complete.

1. $0.5 + \square = 1.3$
2. $0.7 + \square = 1.5$
3. $0.8 + \square = 1.7$
4. $0.4 + \square = 1.2$

5. $\square + 0.9 = 1.4$
6. $\square + 0.6 = 1.3$
7. $\square + 0.7 = 1.6$
8. $\square + 0.9 = 1.5$

9. $1.7 - \square = 0.9$
10. $1.4 - \square = 0.7$
11. $1.5 - \square = 0.6$
12. $1.6 - \square = 0.8$

13. $\square - 0.7 = 0.6$
14. $\square - 0.9 = 0.7$
15. $\square - 0.6 = 0.8$
16. $\square - 0.8 = 0.9$

$$9 - 5 = 4$$

Use the above fact to make other related facts with an answer of:

17. 0.4
18. 1.4
19. 0.04
20. 0.5
21. 0.9
22. 0.15

23. Find five pairs of 3-digit decimals that total 5. You cannot use 0.

TARGET   To use an understanding of place value to +/− large numbers mentally.

Examples

$\underline{27}54 + \underline{9}00 = 3654$

$(27 + 9 = 36)$

$\underline{53}25 - \underline{14}00 = 3925$

$(53 - 14 = 39)$

A

Work out.

1. 163 + 5
2. 328 + 30
3. 179 + 600
4. 245 + 20

5. 530 − 300
6. 426 − 8
7. 871 − 40
8. 904 − 700

9. 353 + 40
10. 115 + 800
11. 764 + 6
12. 429 + 50

13. 622 − 20
14. 140 − 7
15. 898 − 400
16. 133 − 50

17. 637 + 200
18. 208 + 3
19. 561 + 70
20. 356 + 500

21. 182 − 30
22. 449 − 200
23. 925 − 60
24. 600 − 510

B

Work out.

1. 4580 + 700
2. 2197 + 40
3. 1713 + 6000
4. 5438 + 900

5. 1970 − 500
6. 6340 − 80
7. 2126 − 120
8. 3652 − 3050

9. 160 + 2400
10. 5843 + 150
11. 2034 + 3800
12. 1500 + 267

13. 12 329 − 9000
14. 4015 − 600
15. 14 271 − 4200
16. 55 657 − 5007

17. 4916 + 7000
18. 78 + 6002
19. 2060 + 380
20. 703 + 1009

21. 2925 − 1400
22. 10 037 − 8000
23. 3549 − 503
24. 17 256 − 3006

C

Work out.

1. 19 999 + 8000
2. 3864 + 200 000
3. 270 510 + 36 000
4. 102 000 + 5700

5. 65 372 − 400
6. 124 088 − 90 000
7. 721 136 − 20 100
8. 283 560 − 3500

9. 65 004 + 407 000
10. 19 063 + 160
11. 333 500 + 82 000
12. 97 000 + 7030

13. 102 391 − 5000
14. 38 429 − 32 000
15. 43 644 − 640
16. 569 218 − 109 000

17. 13 765 + 407 000
18. 614 416 + 1800
19. 50 050 + 50 050
20. 17 396 + 300 600

21. 295 200 − 1900
22. 10 000 − 720
23. 444 715 − 206 000
24. 208 028 − 58 000

TARGET To add and subtract 2-digit numbers mentally.

Examples

PARTITIONING (+)

$$88 + 64 = 88 + 60 + 4$$
$$= 148 + 4$$
$$= 152$$

or

$$88 + 64 = (80 + 60) + (8 + 4)$$
$$= 140 + 12$$
$$= 152$$

PARTITIONING (−)

$$93 - 56 = 93 - 50 - 6$$
$$= 43 - 6$$
$$= 37$$

or

COUNTING UP

$$93 - 56 \quad 56 \rightarrow 60 = 4$$
$$60 \rightarrow 90 = 30$$
$$90 \rightarrow 93 = 3$$
$$\text{Answer } 37$$

A

Copy and complete.

1. $34 + 23 = \boxed{}$
2. $28 + 44 = \boxed{}$
3. $46 + 35 = \boxed{}$
4. $52 + 29 = \boxed{}$

5. $54 - 22 = \boxed{}$
6. $93 - 53 = \boxed{}$
7. $81 - 37 = \boxed{}$
8. $62 - 28 = \boxed{}$

9. $35 + \boxed{} = 97$
10. $47 + \boxed{} = 88$
11. $\boxed{} + 23 = 74$
12. $\boxed{} + 52 = 86$

13. $79 - \boxed{} = 35$
14. $43 - \boxed{} = 27$
15. $\boxed{} - 34 = 56$
16. $\boxed{} - 45 = 48$

B

Copy and complete.

1. $78 + 53 = \boxed{}$
2. $57 + 47 = \boxed{}$
3. $85 + 48 = \boxed{}$
4. $66 + 76 = \boxed{}$

5. $104 - 58 = \boxed{}$
6. $111 - 29 = \boxed{}$
7. $153 - 77 = \boxed{}$
8. $125 - 66 = \boxed{}$

9. $59 + \boxed{} = 83$
10. $35 + \boxed{} = 72$
11. $\boxed{} + 25 = 91$
12. $\boxed{} + 38 = 66$

13. $82 - \boxed{} = 35$
14. $97 - \boxed{} = 72$
15. $\boxed{} - 27 = 43$
16. $\boxed{} - 48 = 92$

C

Copy and complete.

1. $67 + \boxed{44} = 111$
2. $94 + \boxed{59} = 153$
3. $\boxed{67} + 78 = 145$
4. $\boxed{86} + 45 = 131$

5. $105 - \boxed{66} = 39$
6. $113 - \boxed{59} = 54$
7. $\boxed{151} - 73 = 78$
8. $\boxed{130} - 64 = 66$

9. $55 + \boxed{47} = 102$
10. $89 + \boxed{35} = 124$
11. $\boxed{57} + 76 = 133$
12. $\boxed{97} + 64 = 161$

13. $122 - \boxed{66} = 56$
14. $174 - \boxed{76} = 98$
15. $\boxed{146} - 59 = 87$
16. $\boxed{203} - 98 = 105$

TARGET   To +/− numbers mentally by counting up.

Example

Finding pairs of numbers that add up to 100.

$100 - \boxed{} = 42$

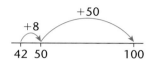

Answer *58*

A

Copy and complete.

1. $10 + \boxed{} = 100$
2. $50 + \boxed{} = 100$
3. $80 + \boxed{} = 100$
4. $30 + \boxed{} = 100$
5. $40 + \boxed{} = 100$
6. $75 + \boxed{} = 100$
7. $15 + \boxed{} = 100$
8. $55 + \boxed{} = 100$
9. $25 + \boxed{} = 100$
10. $65 + \boxed{} = 100$

B

Copy and complete.

1. $100 - 32 = \boxed{}$
2. $100 - 76 = \boxed{}$
3. $100 - 19 = \boxed{}$
4. $100 - 64 = \boxed{}$
5. $100 - 47 = \boxed{}$
6. $100 - \boxed{} = 83$
7. $100 - \boxed{} = 21$
8. $100 - \boxed{} = 56$
9. $100 - \boxed{} = 92$
10. $100 - \boxed{} = 38$

C

Copy and complete.

1. $\boxed{} + 430 = 1000$
2. $\boxed{} + 780 = 1000$
3. $\boxed{} + 520 = 1000$
4. $\boxed{} + 870 = 1000$
5. $\boxed{} + 140 = 1000$
6. $660 + \boxed{} = 1000$
7. $390 + \boxed{} = 1000$
8. $930 + \boxed{} = 1000$
9. $270 + \boxed{} = 1000$
10. $480 + \boxed{} = 1000$

Example

Finding a difference by counting up.

$2005 - 1894$

$1894 \rightarrow 1900 = 6$
$1900 \rightarrow 2000 = 100$
$2000 \rightarrow 2005 = 5$

Answer *111*

A

Work out

1. $43 - 37$
2. $61 - 56$
3. $35 - 28$
4. $50 - 39$
5. $80 - 67$
6. $70 - 54$
7. $100 - 85$
8. $102 - 94$
9. $200 - 191$
10. $200 - 187$

B

Work out

1. $84 - 75$
2. $400 - 382$
3. $2000 - 1996$
4. $303 - 285$
5. $5000 - 4981$
6. $904 - 798$
7. $4002 - 3970$
8. $701 - 493$
9. $6005 - 5986$
10. $806 - 697$

C

Copy and complete.

1. $502 - \boxed{} = 284$
2. $805 - \boxed{} = 673$
3. $913 - \boxed{} = 397$
4. $606 - \boxed{} = 289$
5. $717 - \boxed{} = 495$
6. $2000 - \boxed{} = 781$
7. $4000 - \boxed{} = 1948$
8. $9001 - \boxed{} = 699$
9. $3005 - \boxed{} = 1988$
10. $5012 - \boxed{} = 3975$

TARGET To develop strategies to +/− numbers mentally.

Examples

MAKING 100

$63 + \boxed{} = 100$

$63 \rightarrow 70 = 7$
$70 \rightarrow 100 = 30$
Answer *37*

PARTITIONING

$86 + 55 = 86 + 50 + 5$
$= 136 + 5$
$= 141$

A

Copy and complete.

1. $30 + \boxed{} = 100$
2. $50 + \boxed{} = 100$
3. $90 + \boxed{} = 100$
4. $20 + \boxed{} = 100$
5. $40 + \boxed{} = 100$
6. $70 + \boxed{} = 100$
7. $15 + \boxed{} = 100$
8. $65 + \boxed{} = 100$
9. $25 + \boxed{} = 100$
10. $85 + \boxed{} = 100$
11. $5 + \boxed{} = 100$
12. $55 + \boxed{} = 100$

Work out

13. $28 + 25$
14. $56 + 36$
15. $64 - 27$
16. $93 - 58$
17. $49 + 47$
18. $37 + 25$
19. $85 - 39$
20. $71 - 43$
21. $63 + 19$
22. $46 + 35$
23. $95 - 27$
24. $82 - 46$

B

Copy and complete.

1. $61 + \boxed{} = 100$
2. $38 + \boxed{} = 100$
3. $83 + \boxed{} = 100$
4. $17 + \boxed{} = 100$
5. $54 + \boxed{} = 100$
6. $26 + \boxed{} = 100$
7. $950 + \boxed{} = 1000$
8. $450 + \boxed{} = 1000$
9. $750 + \boxed{} = 1000$
10. $350 + \boxed{} = 1000$
11. $150 + \boxed{} = 1000$
12. $50 + \boxed{} = 1000$

Work out

13. $75 + 39$
14. $86 + 47$
15. $112 - 64$
16. $143 - 78$
17. $93 + 28$
18. $67 + 85$
19. $125 - 39$
20. $160 - 83$
21. $58 + 49$
22. $74 + 97$
23. $101 - 67$
24. $134 - 76$

C

Copy and complete.

1. $730 + \boxed{} = 1000$
2. $260 + \boxed{} = 1000$
3. $810 + \boxed{} = 1000$
4. $490 + \boxed{} = 1000$
5. $970 + \boxed{} = 1000$
6. $120 + \boxed{} = 1000$
7. $640 + \boxed{} = 1000$
8. $380 + \boxed{} = 1000$
9. $530 + \boxed{} = 1000$
10. $760 + \boxed{} = 1000$
11. $410 + \boxed{} = 1000$
12. $870 + \boxed{} = 1000$

Copy and complete.

13. $\boxed{} + 48 = 84$
14. $\boxed{} + 54 = 121$
15. $\boxed{} - 36 = 87$
16. $\boxed{} - 65 = 79$
17. $\boxed{} + 38 = 116$
18. $\boxed{} + 49 = 145$
19. $\boxed{} - 58 = 54$
20. $\boxed{} - 64 = 97$
21. $\boxed{} + 37 = 122$
22. $\boxed{} + 24 = 103$
23. $\boxed{} - 75 = 68$
24. $\boxed{} - 88 = 92$

TARGET   To +/− to the nearest multiple of 10 and adjust.

Examples
$$56 + 29 = 56 + 30 - 1$$
$$= 86 - 1$$
$$= 85$$

$$74 - 39 = 74 - 40 + 1$$
$$= 34 + 1$$
$$= 35$$

A
Work out

1. $45 + 9$
2. $32 - 19$
3. $57 + 21$
4. $88 - 21$
5. $24 + 19$
6. $49 - 19$
7. $35 + 31$
8. $56 - 31$
9. $73 + 19$
10. $38 - 19$

B
Work out

1. $64 + 31$
2. $97 - 39$
3. $82 + 29$
4. $79 - 51$
5. $66 + 41$
6. $184 - 49$
7. $89 + 39$
8. $93 + 51$
9. $155 - 31$
10. $188 - 69$

C
Copy and complete.

1. ☐ $+ 41 = 275$
2. ☐ $- 59 = 327$
3. ☐ $+ 69 = 314$
4. ☐ $- 31 = 683$
5. ☐ $+ 72 = 559$
6. ☐ $- 78 = 174$
7. ☐ $+ 58 = 436$
8. ☐ $- 42 = 783$
9. ☐ $+ 82 = 664$
10. ☐ $- 48 = 297$

TARGET   To +/− by partitioning.

Examples
$$67 + 36 = 67 + 30 + 6$$
$$= 97 + 6$$
$$= 103$$

$$125 - 48 = 125 - 40 - 8$$
$$= 85 - 8$$
$$= 77$$

A
Work out

1. $34 + 45$
2. $27 + 33$
3. $54 + 29$
4. $48 + 46$
5. $35 + 57$
6. $58 - 24$
7. $83 - 35$
8. $62 - 47$
9. $90 - 53$
10. $76 - 28$

B
Work out

1. $86 + 27$
2. $65 + 59$
3. $134 - 67$
4. $113 - 55$
5. $78 + 65$
6. $44 + 88$
7. $145 - 66$
8. $121 - 34$
9. $96 + 36$
10. $152 - 87$

C
Copy and complete.

1. ☐ $+ 36 = 115$
2. ☐ $- 25 = 97$
3. ☐ $+ 47 = 123$
4. ☐ $- 54 = 77$
5. ☐ $+ 88 = 162$
6. ☐ $- 47 = 76$
7. ☐ $+ 59 = 145$
8. ☐ $- 38 = 84$
9. ☐ $+ 67 = 114$
10. ☐ $- 66 = 88$

TARGET To use a variety of strategies to +/− numbers mentally.

A

Write the answers only.

1. 34 − 9
2. 45 + 25
3. 57 + 36
4. 581 − 60
5. 55 + 21
6. 930 − 200
7. 82 − 28
8. 426 + 300
9. 64 − 37
10. 358 + 40
11. 91 − 55
12. 200 − 193
13. 70 − 58
14. 34 + 48
15. 98 − 11
16. 762 − 500

Add 27 to:

17. 47
18. 64
19. 38

Take 8 from:

20. 52
21. 105
22. 87

Make 100:

23. 15
24. 75
25. 45

Add 19 to:

26. 55
27. 23
28. 78

Take 36 from:

29. 63
30. 100
31. 85

B

Write the answers only.

1. 1347 + 6
2. 130 − 52
3. 500 − 5
4. 75 + 38
5. 900 + 6005
6. 2748 − 206
7. 5032 + 4900
8. 6000 − 8
9. 3026 + 44
10. 123 − 68
11. 320 + 7009
12. 9074 − 500
13. 80 + 1040
14. 4785 − 780
15. 154 − 87
16. 76 + 55

Add 3600 to:

17. 7
18. 4008
19. 340

Add 65 to:

20. 79
21. 3040
22. 57

Take 51 from:

23. 85
24. 167
25. 132

Take 47 from:

26. 82
27. 116
28. 143

Make 100:

29. 53 + ☐
30. 26 + ☐
31. 81 + ☐

C

Copy and complete by writing the missing number in the box.

1. 180 + ☐ = 620
2. 910 − ☐ = 540
3. 3003 − ☐ = 1994
4. 374 600 − ☐ = 372 800
5. ☐ + 360 = 740
6. 134 − ☐ = 56
7. 857 − ☐ = 630
8. 25 034 + ☐ = 25 284
9. 4·9 + ☐ = 10·0
10. 7005 − ☐ = 6972
11. 454 + ☐ = 500
12. ☐ + 300 500 = 459 700
13. 850 − ☐ = 490
14. 7·3 + ☐ = 10·0
15. ☐ + 76 = 222
16. 1137 − ☐ = 400
17. 714 + ☐ = 800
18. 62 174 − ☐ = 46 174

TARGET   To add numbers using a written method.

Examples

$$\begin{array}{r} 5\ 2\ 7 \\ +\ 2\ 6\ 8 \\ \hline 7\ 9\ 5 \\ {\scriptstyle 1} \end{array}$$

$$\begin{array}{r} 3\ 8\ 4\ 9 \\ +\ 1\ 5\ 3\ 7 \\ \hline 5\ 3\ 8\ 6 \\ {\scriptstyle 1\ \ \ 1} \end{array}$$

$$\begin{array}{r} 2\ 5\ 3\ 7\ 6 \\ +\ \ \ \ 2\ 6\ 4\ 9 \\ \hline 2\ 8\ 0\ 2\ 5 \\ {\scriptstyle 1\ \ 1\ \ 1} \end{array}$$

A

Copy and complete.

1. $\begin{array}{r} 57 \\ +24 \\ \hline \end{array}$

2. $\begin{array}{r} 62 \\ +36 \\ \hline \end{array}$

3. $\begin{array}{r} 84 \\ +43 \\ \hline \end{array}$

4. $\begin{array}{r} 47 \\ +36 \\ \hline \end{array}$

5. $\begin{array}{r} 91 \\ +59 \\ \hline \end{array}$

6. $\begin{array}{r} 156 \\ +138 \\ \hline \end{array}$

7. $\begin{array}{r} 262 \\ +145 \\ \hline \end{array}$

8. $\begin{array}{r} 484 \\ +154 \\ \hline \end{array}$

9. $\begin{array}{r} 308 \\ +127 \\ \hline \end{array}$

10. $\begin{array}{r} 523 \\ +191 \\ \hline \end{array}$

11. In one hour 274 cars pass the school going one way and 219 going the other way. How many cars pass the school altogether?

12. There are 183 raffle tickets sold from the green book and 159 from the orange book. How many raffle tickets are sold altogether?

13. Small cans weigh 275 g. Large cans weigh 165 g more. What do large cans weigh?

B

Copy and complete.

1. $\begin{array}{r} 1386 \\ +1278 \\ \hline \end{array}$

2. $\begin{array}{r} 2467 \\ +\ 353 \\ \hline \end{array}$

3. $\begin{array}{r} 3596 \\ +\ 462 \\ \hline \end{array}$

4. $\begin{array}{r} 2691 \\ +\ 745 \\ \hline \end{array}$

5. $\begin{array}{r} 4587 \\ +4256 \\ \hline \end{array}$

6. $\begin{array}{r} 2243 \\ +1587 \\ \hline \end{array}$

7. $\begin{array}{r} 4656 \\ +2391 \\ \hline \end{array}$

8. $\begin{array}{r} 3715 \\ +2748 \\ \hline \end{array}$

9. $\begin{array}{r} 4589 \\ +3239 \\ \hline \end{array}$

10. $\begin{array}{r} 5974 \\ +3494 \\ \hline \end{array}$

11. There are 3767 children and 2539 adults at a concert. How many people are there at the concert altogether.

12. There are 7496 trees in a forest. 1286 new trees are planted. How many trees are there in the forest now?

13. A vineyard produces 2758 bottles of white wine and 1946 bottles of red wine. How many bottles does it produce altogether?

C

Set out as in the examples.

1. 24 769 + 3753

2. 38 672 + 15 698

3. 56 958 + 3774

4. 75 497 + 23 586

5. 49 835 + 5676

6. 37 583 + 27 897

7. 68 346 + 14 978

8. 86 795 + 3575

9. 57 867 + 26 594

10. 49 489 + 14 682

11. 68 953 + 27 698

12. 36 476 + 35 989

13. Emma has £32 495 in her savings account. She pays in £2839. How much is in her account now?

14. In one day 54 806 passengers arrive at an airport and 29 325 depart. How many people pass through the airport?

TARGET To practise using a written method to add.

Examples

```
    1 9 3 4          7 2 4 5          6 5 0 7 8
  +   6 8 7        + 1 7 9 3        + 1 5 4 3 9
    2 6 2 1          9 0 3 8          8 0 5 1 7
    1 1 1              1 1            1   1 1
```

A

Copy and complete.

1. 148 + 128

2. 357 + 235

3. 272 + 166

4. 659 + 117

5. 491 + 238

6. 385 + 167

7. 568 + 353

8. 454 + 247

9. 797 + 148

10. 576 + 234

11. A newsagent sells 272 papers in the morning and 155 in the afternoon. How many papers are sold altogether?

12. There are 196 cars in a car park. 146 more come in. How many cars are in the car park now?

13. A cinema audience is made up of 256 children and 149 adults. How many people are watching the film?

B

Copy and complete.

1. 4652 + 3837

2. 2389 + 1543

3. 4925 + 2635

4. 3270 + 1456

5. 2517 + 1869

6. 5494 + 3645

7. 4736 + 1786

8. 7163 + 1457

9. 6841 + 2975

10. 3678 + 2786

11. A dairy produces 2685 litres of full fat milk and 1347 litres of skimmed milk. How many litres of milk is produced altogether?

12. The mileage of a car is 7479 miles. In the next month it is driven a further 1962 miles. What is the mileage now?

13. In April a plumber earns £3165. In May he earns £2798. How much has he earned in the two months combined?

C

Set out as in the examples.

1. 14 873 + 17 548

2. 43 249 + 15 965

3. 32 768 + 27 857

4. 71 956 + 8478

5. 22 475 + 25 895

6. 56 837 + 12 393

7. 48 394 + 6769

8. 31 592 + 18 838

9. 63 868 + 16 746

10. 52 978 + 38 872

11. A clothes shop makes a profit in one year of £81 537. In the following year its profit increases by £14 925. What is the profit in the second year?

12. The winning candidate in an election polls 46 915 votes. The other three candidates poll 37 396 votes altogether. How many people voted in the election?

13. The first edition of a magazine sells 38 429 copies. The second edition sells 17 648 more copies than the first How many copies of the second edition are sold?

TARGET   To subtract numbers using a written method.

Examples

```
    4  1
    5̶  3  7
 -  3  5  4
 ───────────
    1  8  3
```

```
  0  1  8  16  1
  1̶  4  9̶  7̶  1
 -    7  2  9  5
 ──────────────
      7  6  7  6
```

```
  8  1  7  11  1
  9̶  3  8̶  2̶  0
 -  2  4  6  7  5
 ──────────────
    6  9  1  4  5
```

A

Copy and complete.

1. 583
    − 256

2. 329
    − 172

3. 764
    − 146

4. 815
    − 385

5. 493
    − 259

6. 757
    − 482

7. 246
    − 127

8. 825
    − 684

9. 593
    − 137

10. 610
    − 268

11. There are 240 tea bags in a packet. 107 are used. How many tea bags are left?

12. There are 345 caravans at a site. 183 are empty. How many have people staying in them?

B

Copy and complete.

1. 1736
    − 1473

2. 3194
    − 2520

3. 4859
    − 1665

4. 2483
    − 1939

5. 8567
    − 3387

6. 7427
    − 4945

7. 5940
    − 1787

8. 9065
    − 2829

9. 7628
    − 1772

10. 4055
    − 3627

11. Of the 2736 people who use a swimming pool in one month, 1258 are children. How many are adults?

12. 5218 people live in Westdean. 3935 people live in Eastdean. How many more people live in Westdean than in Eastdean?

13. In November a shop sells 4371 cards. In December 2648 are sold. How many more cards are sold in November than December?

C

Copy and complete.

1. 15927
    − 3645

2. 18163
    − 5723

3. 23742
    − 9619

4. 22958
    − 16370

5. 45645
    − 24792

6. 73286
    − 14523

7. 34714
    − 16356

8. 54329
    − 42685

9. 81560
    − 33843

10. 62071
    − 27156

11. 48145
    − 16479

12. 93690
    − 57848

13. At the start of the year Ishaan has £17 585 in his savings account. By the end of the year he has £21 349. By how much have his savings increased?

14. A dairy produces 52 460 kg of butter and 29 503 kg of cheese. How much more butter is produced than cheese?

TARGET To practise using a written method to subtract.

Examples

$$
\begin{array}{r}
{\scriptstyle 7\ \ 11\ \ 1} \\
8\ 2\ 5 \\
-\ 2\ 3\ 8 \\
\hline
5\ 8\ 7
\end{array}
\qquad
\begin{array}{r}
{\scriptstyle 6\ \ 1\ \ 4\ \ 1} \\
7\ 2\ 5\ 6 \\
-\ 4\ 9\ 3\ 8 \\
\hline
2\ 3\ 1\ 8
\end{array}
\qquad
\begin{array}{r}
{\scriptstyle 3\ \ 12\ \ 1\ \ 6\ \ 1} \\
4\ 3\ 1\ 7\ 4 \\
-\ \ \ 6\ 8\ 2\ 5 \\
\hline
3\ 6\ 3\ 4\ 9
\end{array}
$$

A

Copy and complete.

1	229 − 153	7	336 − 259
2	363 − 148	8	813 − 327
3	647 − 361	9	524 − 268
4	452 − 139	10	941 − 495
5	716 − 572	11	440 − 274
6	548 − 129	12	752 − 364

13 A school buys 248 exercise books. 175 are used. How many are left?

14 There are 472 passengers on a ferry to France. 219 fewer people make the return journey. How many passengers are on the ferry to England?

B

Copy and complete.

1	2386 − 1571	7	9365 − 8285
2	4528 − 1964	8	8270 − 3497
3	5142 − 3650	9	5341 − 2868
4	6623 − 5296	10	7612 − 2647
5	7419 − 4835	11	6430 − 4978
6	3274 − 1459	12	9281 − 4346

13 A plane is flying 4191 miles from London to Delhi. It has flown 2738 miles. How much further is the flight?

C

Copy and complete.

1	23749 − 1357	7	22974 − 15556
2	15273 − 2468	8	73463 − 36973
3	31485 − 12514	9	62752 − 46808
4	56358 − 31773	10	41306 − 18592
5	85861 − 28557	11	96931 − 57484
6	47632 − 41980	12	30418 − 15754

13 A car has a price of £12960. In a sale Una buys it for £8799. How much has she saved?

14 A crowd of 51429 watch City's football match on Saturday. 14653 fewer spectators see their game on Tuesday. What is the Tuesday game's attendance?

TARGET To practise a written method for addition and subtraction.

Examples

```
    3 5 7 8
  + 2 4 9 4
    6 0 7 2
    1 1 1
```

```
    7  12 10  1
    8  3  1  5
  - 4  3  5  7
    3  9  5  8
```

A

Copy and complete.

1)   236
   + 158

2)   392
   + 267

3)   545
   + 147

4)   480
   + 356

5)   324
   + 139

6)   673
   + 243

7)   471
   − 126

8)   348
   − 165

9)   563
   − 247

10)   259
   − 183

11)   650
   − 324

12)   427
   − 291

13) There are 336 pupils in a school. 172 are boys. How many girls are in the school?

14) In an orchard 529 red apples and 347 green apples are picked. How many apples are picked altogether?

15) A plane is flying at 580 metres above ground level. A tower, 235 metres tall, is directly below the plane. How much distance is there between the plane and the top of the tower?

B

Copy and complete.

1)   1548
   + 674

2)   2375
   + 1685

3)   3867
   + 3675

4)   7639
   + 1878

5)   5486
   + 2529

6)   4953
   + 1789

7)   5835
   − 956

8)   3152
   − 2457

9)   4416
   − 1928

10)   8524
   − 3765

11)   6273
   − 2374

12)   7340
   − 4837

13) A farmer has 2361 sheep. 1485 have been sheared. How many have not been sheared?

14) Each month Mrs Jones earns £3689 and Mr Jones earns £2792. How much do they earn in a month altogether?

15) A bookshop sells 5768 books in one week and 8420 books in the next week. How many more books are sold in the second week?

C

Copy and complete.

1)   43 687
   + 28 576

2)   55 894
   + 34 958

3)   27 358
   + 17 693

4)   34 976
   + 26 596

5)   59 735
   + 49 376

6)   68 469
   + 18 734

7)   65 341
   − 19 685

8)   81 630
   − 57 695

9)   53 257
   − 33 549

10)   72 513
   − 26 837

11)   46 425
   − 39 447

12)   94 182
   − 57 988

13) Santa Claus has 53 740 toys. He delivers 38 593. How many toys does he have left?

14) A factory makes 84 597 radios in a year. In the next year production goes up by 15 835. How many radios are made in the second year?

TARGET   To practise a written method for addition and subtraction.

Examples

```
    4 9 3 6
  + 2 1 8 9
  ─────────
    7 1 2 5
    1 1 1
```

```
   5  11  16  1
   6   2   7  4
 − 1   6   7  7
 ──────────────
   4   5   9  7
```

A

Copy and complete.

1.   563
     + 287

2.   457
     + 146

3.   629
     + 273

4.   585
     + 317

5.   248
     + 242

6.   396
     + 262

7.   582
     − 276

8.   219
     − 155

9.   673
     − 348

10.   420
      − 152

11.   754
      − 586

12.   947
      − 492

13. A Primary School has 415 pupils. 236 of the children are in the Upper School. How many are in the Lower School?

14. A lorry driver travels 436 miles. He still has 279 miles to drive. How long is his journey?

15. Norman's book has 308 pages. He has read 242 pages. How many more does he still have to read?

B

Copy and complete.

1.   4795
     + 4294

2.   5876
     + 2384

3.   2264
     + 1799

4.   3548
     + 1475

5.   6687
     + 2729

6.   4749
     + 3555

7.   3271
     − 976

8.   8453
     − 4467

9.   5630
     − 3057

10.   7142
      − 2283

11.   4315
      − 3495

12.   6524
      − 4775

13. The Nile is 4160 miles long. The Yangtze is 3915 miles long. What is the difference in the lengths of the rivers?

14. In July 5639 people visit a zoo. In August the number of visitors goes up by 2485. How many people visit the zoo in August?

C

Copy and complete.

1.   41 636
     + 27 689

2.   29 578
     + 28 376

3.   57 785
     + 13 295

4.   76 947
     + 13 486

5.   33 869
     + 27 587

6.   65 394
     + 19 669

7.   23 126
     − 3479

8.   61 532
     − 21 598

9.   95 344
     − 79 768

10.   82 063
      − 64 866

11.   36 410
      − 20 785

12.   74 205
      − 15 237

13. In one day a road is used by 69 284 cars and 25 796 other vehicles. How many vehicles use the road altogether?

14. There are 31 276 runners in a marathon. 5718 are wearing fancy dress. How many are not wearing fancy dress?

15. The population of Downton is 81 425. Upton's population is 68 569. How many more people live in Downton than Upton?

TARGET To estimate answers by rounding and to check answers using inverse operations.

Examples

ESTIMATING ANSWERS

3584 + 2538

3600 + 2500 = 6100

Answer is approximately 6100

4786 − 2579

4800 − 2600 = 2200

Answer is approximately 2200

CHECKING ANSWERS

```
    3 5 8 4
  + 2 5 3 8
    6 1 2 2
    1   1   1
```

```
  5 10 11  1
    6  X  2  2
  - 2  5  3  8
    3  5  8  4
```

The answer of 3584 matches the original calculation.

```
        7  1
    4 7 8 6
  - 2 5 7 9
    2 2 0 7
```

```
    2 2 0 7
  + 2 5 7 9
    4 7 8 6
          1
```

The answer of 4786 matches the original calculation.

A

Estimate and then work out.

1 43 + 36

2 81 + 62

3 155 + 29

4 78 + 24

5 96 − 25

6 83 − 34

7 48 − 22

8 151 − 67

Work out and then check the answer.

9 62 + 47

10 75 + 54

11 126 − 68

12 153 − 81

13 450 + 320

14 580 + 290

15 730 − 470

16 910 − 540

B

Estimate and then work out.

1 164 + 87

2 288 + 41

3 112 − 73

4 439 − 55

5 4533 + 1620

6 2870 + 2435

7 7965 − 258

8 4310 − 2890

Work out and then check the answer.

9 384 + 247

10 429 + 353

11 672 − 161

12 919 − 590

13 2072 + 1830

14 6940 + 2756

15 9135 − 3727

16 7381 − 4869

C

Estimate and then work out.

1 1745 + 423

2 2137 + 568

3 1482 − 359

4 3026 − 975

5 14 290 + 2550

6 16 725 + 1473

7 15 609 − 2235

8 19 183 − 3861

Work out and then check the answer.

9 1479 + 736

10 3692 + 417

11 5235 − 638

12 2497 − 864

13 30 580 + 5177

14 21 854 + 8749

15 19 236 − 4392

16 54 960 − 7653

TARGET   To solve number problems involving mental addition and subtraction.

In a magic square the sum of each row, column and diagonal is the same.

20	11	17
13	16	19
15	21	12

Example

Row	$13 + 16 + 19 = 48$
Column	$17 + 19 + 12 = 48$
Diagonal	$15 + 16 + 17 = 48$

Copy and complete the following magic squares.

A

1

		11
		2
	10	8

2

2	9	16
		4

3

		6
	12	
18		10

4

		8
15	10	23

B

1

21		
	20	
	16	19

2

9		
24		12
21		

3

19	17	33
37		

4

		28
	25	
22		18

C

1

3		−1
	0	
		−3

2

−3		
4	−1	0

3

	0	5
		−2
		3

4

−2		
9	1	−7

TARGET To solve number puzzles involving addition and subtraction.

In an addition pyramid, pairs of numbers
are added together to make the number above them.

Example

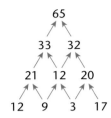

```
            65
          ↗   ↖
        33      32
       ↗ ↖    ↗ ↖
     21    12    20
    ↗↖   ↗↖   ↗↖
   12   9    3    17
```

Copy and complete the following addition pyramids.

A

1.
```
       ☐
     ☐   ☐
    6   9   3
```

2.
```
      ☐
    14   ☐
   10  ☐   7
```

3.
```
      35
    ☐   ☐
   5   8   ☐
```

4.
```
      37
    ☐   21
   ☐  ☐   9
```

5.
```
      ☐
   26   17
    ☐  11  ☐
```

6.
```
      50
    30   ☐
   ☐  ☐   13
```

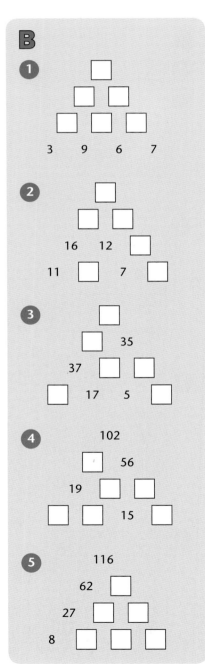

B

1.
```
        ☐
      ☐   ☐
    ☐   ☐   ☐
   3   9   6   7
```

2.
```
         ☐
       ☐   ☐
     16  12   ☐
   11  ☐   7   ☐
```

3.
```
         ☐
       ☐   35
     37  ☐   ☐
   ☐  17   5   ☐
```

4.
```
        102
       ☐   56
     19  ☐   ☐
   ☐  ☐   15   ☐
```

5.
```
        116
      62   ☐
    27  ☐   ☐
   8  ☐  ☐   ☐
```

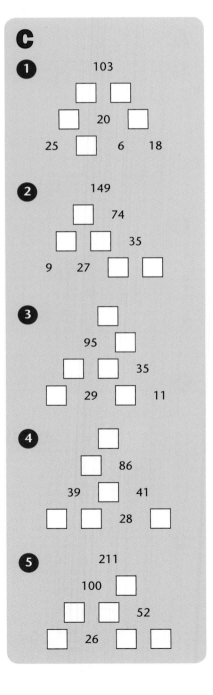

C

1.
```
         103
       ☐   ☐
     ☐   20   ☐
   25  ☐   6   18
```

2.
```
         149
       ☐   74
     ☐   ☐   35
   9  27  ☐   ☐
```

3.
```
          ☐
       95   ☐
     ☐   ☐   35
   ☐  29   ☐  11
```

4.
```
          ☐
        ☐   86
     39   ☐   41
   ☐  ☐   28   ☐
```

5.
```
         211
      100   ☐
     ☐  ☐   52
   ☐  26   ☐
```

TARGET   To solve number puzzles involving addition and subtraction.

In these triangular arithmagons
the pairs of numbers at the end
of each side are added together
to give the number between them.

Example

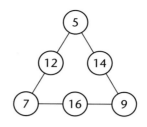

5 + 7 = 12
7 + 9 = 16
9 + 5 = 14

Find the missing numbers in these arithmagons.

A

1

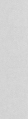

3
A   B
5 — C — 4

2

E
F   11
2 — D — 6

3

4
10   K
L — M — 2

4

Q
8   12
P — 10 — R

B

1

S
15   14
U — 17 — T

2

X
18   11
Z — 15 — Y

3

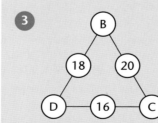

B
18   20
D — 16 — C

4

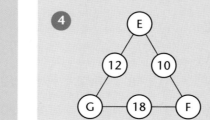

E
12   10
G — 18 — F

C

1

K
23   32
J — 27 — L

2

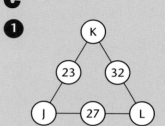

N
34   28
M — 36 — P

3

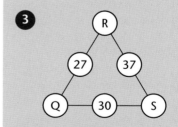

R
27   37
Q — 30 — S

4

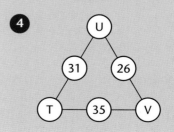

U
31   26
T — 35 — V

TARGET   To recall and use known multiplication facts.

A

What is:

1. 2×10 20
2. 6×2 12
3. 3×5 15
4. 10×10 100
5. $55 \div 5$ 11
6. $18 \div 2$ 8
7. $90 \div 10$ 9
8. $35 \div 5$ 7
9. 8×2 16
10. 12×5 60
11. 11×10 110
12. 4×2 8
13. $80 \div 10$ 8
14. $25 \div 5$ 5
15. $14 \div 2$ 7
16. $120 \div 10$ 12
17. 9×5 45
18. 7×10 70
19. 11×2 22
20. 6×5 30
21. $10 \div 2$ 5
22. $10 \div 10$ 1
23. $40 \div 5$ 8
24. $24 \div 2$ 12

B

Copy and complete.

1. $\square \times 2 = 16$ 8
2. $\square \times 5 = 45$ 9
3. $\square \div 10 = 12$ 120
4. $\square \div 2 = 7$ 14
5. $\square \times 10 = 60$ 6
6. $\square \times 2 = 22$ 11
7. $\square \div 5 = 8$ 40
8. $\square \div 10 = 5$ 50
9. $\square \times 5 = 60$ 12
10. $\square \times 10 = 100$ 10
11. $\square \div 2 = 10$ 20
12. $\square \div 5 = 11$ 55

Write the answer only.

13. 5×3
14. 6×4 24
15. 7×8 56
16. 10×3 30
17. 11×4 44
18. 8×8 64
19. 12×3 36
20. 5×4 20
21. 4×8 32
22. 7×3 21
23. 8×4 32
24. 12×8 96

25. $24 \div 3$ 8
26. $36 \div 4$ 9
27. $48 \div 8$ 6
28. $33 \div 3$ 11
29. $28 \div 4$ 7
30. $40 \div 8$ 5
31. $27 \div 3$ 9
32. $16 \div 4$ 4
33. $88 \div 8$ 11
34. $18 \div 3$ 6
35. $48 \div 4$ 12
36. $72 \div 8$ 9

C

Copy and complete.

1. $\square \times 3 = 15$ 5
2. $\square \times 4 = 40$ 10
3. $\square \div 8 = 5$ 40
4. $\square \div 3 = 8$ 24
5. $\square \times 8 = 8$ 1
6. $\square \times 3 = 36$ 12
7. $\square \div 4 = 5$ 20
8. $\square \div 8 = 7$ 56
9. $\square \times 4 = 12$ 3
10. $\square \times 8 = 72$ 9
11. $\square \div 3 = 1$ 3
12. $\square \div 4 = 11$ 44

Write the answer only.

13. 90×3 270
14. 70×4 280
15. 110×8 880
16. 60×3 180
17. 40×4 160
18. 30×8 270
19. 80×3 240
20. 90×4 360
21. 60×8 480
22. 110×3 330
23. 120×4 480
24. 90×8 720

25. $300 \div 3$ 100
26. $240 \div 4$ 60
27. $640 \div 8$ 80
28. $120 \div 3$ 40
29. $440 \div 4$ 110
30. $320 \div 8$ 40
31. $360 \div 3$ 120
32. $280 \div 4$ 70
33. $800 \div 8$ 100
34. $210 \div 3$ 70
35. $320 \div 4$ 80
36. $960 \div 8$ 120

TARGET   To recall and use ×/÷ facts for the 6 times table.

A

Work out

1 3×6
2 7×6
3 5×6
4 10×6

5 2×6
6 9×6
7 4×6
8 12×6

9 0×6
10 8×6
11 1×6
12 6×6

13 $30 \div 6$
14 $54 \div 6$
15 $24 \div 6$
16 $42 \div 6$

17 $66 \div 6$
18 $6 \div 6$
19 $12 \div 6$
20 $36 \div 6$

21 $60 \div 6$
22 $18 \div 6$
23 $48 \div 6$
24 $72 \div 6$

B

Copy and complete.

1 $\square \times 6 = 24$
2 $\square \times 6 = 36$
3 $\square \div 6 = 10$
4 $\square \div 6 = 8$

5 $\square \times 6 = 6$
6 $\square \times 6 = 48$
7 $\square \div 6 = 11$
8 $\square \div 6 = 5$

9 $\square \times 6 = 30$
10 $\square \times 6 = 72$
11 $\square \div 6 = 4$
12 $\square \div 6 = 6$

13 $\square \times 6 = 54$
14 $\square \times 6 = 0$
15 $\square \div 6 = 2$
16 $\square \div 6 = 9$

17 $\square \times 6 = 18$
18 $\square \times 6 = 42$
19 $\square \div 6 = 7$
20 $\square \div 6 = 12$

21 Each seat on a coach costs £6. How many seats can be bought for:
a) £48   b) £120   c) £66?

C

Work out

1 20×6
2 80×6
3 120×6
4 70×6

5 30×6
6 60×6
7 40×6
8 90×6

9 $180 \div 6$
10 $600 \div 6$
11 $360 \div 6$
12 $660 \div 6$

13 $420 \div 6$
14 $540 \div 6$
15 $300 \div 6$
16 $480 \div 6$

Work out by multiplying by 6 and doubling.

17 4×12
18 7×12
19 12×12
20 9×12

21 5×12
22 8×12
23 3×12
24 6×12

Work out by halving and dividing by 6.

25 $60 \div 12$
26 $84 \div 12$
27 $24 \div 12$
28 $108 \div 12$

29 $48 \div 12$
30 $96 \div 12$
31 $36 \div 12$
32 $72 \div 12$

33 There are 12 paper clips in each packet. How many paper clips are there in:
a) 12 packets
b) 15 packets
c) 40 packets?

TARGET To recall and use ×/÷ facts for the 7 times table.

A

What is:

1. 2×7
2. 6×7
3. 4×7
4. 8×7

5. 11×7
6. 5×7
7. 3×7
8. 9×7

9. 0×7
10. 7×7
11. 10×7
12. 12×7

13. $21 \div 7$
14. $56 \div 7$
15. $35 \div 7$
16. $70 \div 7$

17. $84 \div 7$
18. $49 \div 7$
19. $7 \div 7$
20. $42 \div 7$

21. $63 \div 7$
22. $28 \div 7$
23. $77 \div 7$
24. $14 \div 7$

B

Copy and complete.

1. $\square \times 7 = 28$
2. $\square \times 7 = 49$
3. $\square \times 7 = 84$
4. $\square \times 7 = 63$

5. $\square \times 7 = 0$
6. $\square \times 7 = 42$
7. $\square \times 7 = 21$
8. $\square \times 7 = 35$

9. $\square \times 7 = 7$
10. $\square \times 7 = 56$
11. $\square \times 7 = 14$
12. $\square \times 7 = 77$

13. $\square \div 7 = 6$
14. $\square \div 7 = 10$
15. $\square \div 7 = 1$
16. $\square \div 7 = 8$

17. $\square \div 7 = 3$
18. $\square \div 7 = 7$
19. $\square \div 7 = 11$
20. $\square \div 7 = 5$

21. $\square \div 7 = 2$
22. $\square \div 7 = 9$
23. $\square \div 7 = 4$
24. $\square \div 7 = 12$

C

Write the answers only.

1. 20×7
2. 50×7
3. 90×7
4. 60×7

5. 110×7
6. 80×7
7. 40×7
8. 70×7

9. $210 \div 7$
10. $560 \div 7$
11. $840 \div 7$
12. $350 \div 7$

13. $490 \div 7$
14. $280 \div 7$
15. $630 \div 7$
16. $420 \div 7$

Work out by multiplying by 7 and doubling.

17. 2×14
18. 6×14
19. 3×14
20. 7×14

21. 5×14
22. 9×14
23. 11×14
24. 8×14

How many days make:

25. 8 weeks
26. 12 weeks
27. 21 weeks
28. 52 weeks.

How many weeks make:

29. 42 days
30. 91 days
31. 147 days
32. 245 days.

TARGET To recall and use ×/÷ facts for the 9 times table.

A

Work out

1. 3 × 9   24
2. 6 × 9   54
3. 10 × 9   90
4. 9 × 9   81
5. 11 × 9   99
6. 5 × 9   45
7. 0 × 9   0
8. 8 × 9   72
9. 1 × 9   9
10. 12 × 9   108
11. 4 × 9   36
12. 7 × 9   63
13. 45 ÷ 9   5
14. 81 ÷ 9   9
15. 18 ÷ 9   2
16. 99 ÷ 9   11
17. 36 ÷ 9   4
18. 63 ÷ 9   7
19. 90 ÷ 9   10
20. 108 ÷ 9   12
21. 27 ÷ 9   3
22. 72 ÷ 9   8
23. 9 ÷ 9   1
24. 54 ÷ 9   6

B

Copy and complete.

1. ☐2 × 9 = 18
2. ☐7 × 9 = 63
3. ☐4 × 9 = 36
4. ☐10 × 9 = 90
5. ☐1 × 9 = 9
6. ☐6 × 9 = 54
7. ☐9 × 9 = 81
8. ☐5 × 9 = 45
9. ☐3 × 9 = 27
10. ☐12 × 9 = 108
11. ☐0 × 9 = 0
12. ☐8 × 9 = 72
13. ☐63 ÷ 9 = 7
14. ☐90 ÷ 9 = 10
15. ☐18 ÷ 9 = 2
16. ☐81 ÷ 9 = 9
17. ☐27 ÷ 9 = 3
18. ☐99 ÷ 9 = 11
19. ☐45 ÷ 9 = 5
20. ☐54 ÷ 9 = 6
21. ☐36 ÷ 9 = 4
22. ☐9 ÷ 9 = 1
23. ☐72 ÷ 9 = 8
24. ☐108 ÷ 9 = 12

C

Work out

1. 50 × 9   450
2. 90 × 9   810
3. 20 × 9   180
4. 110 × 9   990
5. 80 × 9   720
6. 100 × 9   900
7. 30 × 9   270
8. 70 × 9   630
9. 10 × 9   90
10. 40 × 9   360
11. 120 × 9   1080
12. 60 × 9   540
13. 270 ÷ 9   30
14. 630 ÷ 9   70
15. 90 ÷ 9   10
16. 810 ÷ 9   90
17. 360 ÷ 9   40
18. 540 ÷ 9   60
19. 900 ÷ 9   100
20. 1080 ÷ 9   120
21. 180 ÷ 9   20
22. 720 ÷ 9   80
23. 450 ÷ 9   50
24. 990 ÷ 9   110

25. A coach carries 64 passengers. Tickets cost £9 each. How much is made from ticket sales?   ✗ 64 × 9 = 576   £576

26. Each sandbag weighs 9 kg. What is the total weight of 37 sandbags?   ✗ 37 × 9 = 333 kg

27. There are 72 people bathing in the sea. Nine times as many are on the beach. How many people are on the beach?   ✗ 72 × 9 = 648 people

TARGET   To recall and use known ×/÷ facts.

A
What is:

1. 4×6
2. 5×9
3. 6×2
4. 9×7
5. 8×10
6. 6×8
7. 7×9
8. 9×0
9. 9×6
10. 4×8
11. 9×4
12. 7×7
13. $27 \div 9$
14. $40 \div 5$
15. $42 \div 6$
16. $72 \div 8$
17. $24 \div 3$
18. $56 \div 7$
19. $48 \div 6$
20. $24 \div 4$
21. $81 \div 9$
22. $12 \div 1$
23. $28 \div 7$
24. $64 \div 8$

B
Copy and complete.

1. $\square \times 7 = 42$
2. $\square \times 4 = 32$
3. $\square \times 9 = 45$
4. $\square \times 6 = 54$
5. $\square \times 3 = 18$
6. $\square \times 8 = 56$
7. $\square \div 9 = 4$
8. $\square \div 10 = 7$
9. $\square \div 7 = 8$
10. $\square \div 8 = 9$
11. $\square \div 1 = 5$
12. $\square \div 6 = 3$

Write the answer only.

13. 5×80
14. 8×20
15. 6×90
16. 3×70
17. 7×40
18. 8×60
19. 90×9
20. 70×3
21. 50×7
22. 90×5
23. 80×0
24. 70×6
25. $490 \div 7$
26. $720 \div 9$
27. $180 \div 2$
28. $480 \div 8$
29. $300 \div 6$
30. $360 \div 4$
31. $630 \div 9$
32. $270 \div 3$
33. $360 \div 6$
34. $350 \div 5$
35. $630 \div 7$
36. $240 \div 8$

C
Copy and complete.

1. $\square \div 6 = 90$
2. $\square \div 3 = 80$
3. $\square \div 8 = 40$
4. $\square \div 70 = 6$
5. $\square \div 20 = 7$
6. $\square \div 90 = 5$
7. $\square \times 5 = 300$
8. $\square \times 8 = 400$
9. $\square \times 6 = 480$
10. $\square \times 40 = 240$
11. $\square \times 90 = 810$
12. $\square \times 70 = 210$

Write the answer only.

13. 6×800
14. 8×500
15. 7×900
16. 500×6
17. 600×3
18. 900×0
19. 8×900
20. 6×200
21. 7×800
22. 800×4
23. 700×7
24. 600×6
25. $2700 \div 9$
26. $3500 \div 5$
27. $5600 \div 7$
28. $1600 \div 2$
29. $7200 \div 8$
30. $2400 \div 6$
31. $2800 \div 4$
32. $3500 \div 7$
33. $5400 \div 9$
34. $2100 \div 3$
35. $4200 \div 6$
36. $6400 \div 8$

TARGET   To recall and use ×/÷ facts for the 11 times table.

A

Work out

1. 2 × 11
2. 9 × 11
3. 5 × 11
4. 11 × 11

5. 8 × 11
6. 1 × 11
7. 10 × 11
8. 6 × 11

9. 4 × 11
10. 0 × 11
11. 12 × 11
12. 7 × 11

13. 33 ÷ 11
14. 66 ÷ 11
15. 55 ÷ 11
16. 121 ÷ 11

17. 88 ÷ 11
18. 22 ÷ 11
19. 132 ÷ 11
20. 44 ÷ 11

21. 77 ÷ 11
22. 110 ÷ 11
23. 11 ÷ 11
24. 99 ÷ 11

B

Copy and complete.

1. ☐ × 11 = 33
2. ☐ × 11 = 88
3. ☐ × 11 = 66
4. ☐ × 11 = 110

5. ☐ × 11 = 132
6. ☐ × 11 = 22
7. ☐ × 11 = 0
8. ☐ × 11 = 99

9. ☐ × 11 = 44
10. ☐ × 11 = 11
11. ☐ × 11 = 77
12. ☐ × 11 = 121

13. ☐ ÷ 11 = 5
14. ☐ ÷ 11 = 9
15. ☐ ÷ 11 = 1
16. ☐ ÷ 11 = 12

17. ☐ ÷ 11 = 4
18. ☐ ÷ 11 = 8
19. ☐ ÷ 11 = 3
20. ☐ ÷ 11 = 10

21. ☐ ÷ 11 = 7
22. ☐ ÷ 11 = 11
23. ☐ ÷ 11 = 2
24. ☐ ÷ 11 = 6

C

Work out

1. 40 × 11
2. 70 × 11
3. 20 × 11
4. 90 × 11

5. 0 × 11
6. 80 × 11
7. 50 × 11
8. 110 × 11

9. 30 × 11
10. 100 × 11
11. 60 × 11
12. 120 × 11

13. 550 ÷ 11
14. 880 ÷ 11
15. 110 ÷ 11
16. 1210 ÷ 11

17. 330 ÷ 11
18. 660 ÷ 11
19. 990 ÷ 11
20. 440 ÷ 11

21. 220 ÷ 11
22. 1100 ÷ 11
23. 1320 ÷ 11
24. 770 ÷ 11

25. Sixteen 11-a-side football teams are playing on the eight pitches in a park. How many footballers are playing at the same time?

26. If 319 chairs are arranged equally in 11 rows how many chairs are there in each row?

27. One eleventh of the 506 babies born in a hospital in one year were born in December. How many babies were born in December?

TARGET To recall and use ×/÷ facts for the 12 times table.

A

Work out

1. 7×12
2. 3×12
3. 5×12
4. 9×12

5. 6×12
6. 2×12
7. 0×12
8. 12×12

9. 10×12
10. 8×12
11. 11×12 /32
12. 4×12 48

13. $72 \div 12$ 6
14. $12 \div 12$ 1
15. $60 \div 12$ 5
16. $96 \div 12$ 8

17. $36 \div 12$ 3
18. $120 \div 12$ 10
19. $108 \div 12$ 9
20. $132 \div 12$ 11

21. $24 \div 12$ 2
22. $84 \div 12$ 7
23. $48 \div 12$ 4
24. $144 \div 12$ 12

B

Copy and complete.

1. ☐ $\times 12 = 36$
2. 8 $\times 12 = 96$
3. 10 $\times 12 = 120$
4. 4 $\times 12 = 48$

5. 7 $\times 12 = 84$
6. 1 $\times 12 = 12$
7. 5 $\times 12 = 60$
8. 12 $\times 12 = 144$

9. 0 $\times 12 = 0$
10. 6 $\times 12 = 72$
11. 11 $\times 12 = 132$
12. 9 $\times 12 = 108$

13. 96 $\div 12 = 8$
14. 48 $\div 12 = 4$
15. 12 $\div 12 = 1$
16. 84 $\div 12 = 7$

17. 120 $\div 12 = 10$
18. 24 $\div 12 = 2$
19. 132 $\div 12 = 11$
20. 60 $\div 12 = 5$

21. 72 $\div 12 = 6$
22. 36 $\div 12 = 3$
23. 144 $\div 12 = 12$
24. 108 $\div 12 = 9$

C

Work out

1. 70×12 840
2. 40×12 48
3. 0×12 0
4. 110×12 1320
5. 20×12 240
6. 50×12 60
7. 90×12 1080
8. 100×12 1200
9. 80×12 960
10. 30×12 360
11. 120×12 1440
12. 60×12 720

13. $1080 \div 12$ 90
14. $600 \div 12$ 50
15. $120 \div 12$ 1
16. $840 \div 12$ 70
17. $480 \div 12$ 40
18. $1320 \div 12$ 110
19. $720 \div 12$ 60
20. $240 \div 12$ 20
21. $1200 \div 12$ 100
22. $960 \div 12$ 80
23. $360 \div 12$ 30
24. $1440 \div 12$ 120

25. There are 12 pencils in each box. How many boxes can be made from 312 pencils? 312 × 12 =

26. Desirée saves £75 per month. How much does she save in a year? 75 × 12 =

27. Before 1971 twelve pennies made one shilling.
    a) How many pennies made 18 shillings?
    b) How many shillings was 180 pennies?

28. Work out by multiplying by 12 and doubling:
    a) 6×24 140
    b) 9×24 216
    c) 12×24 188
    d) 51×24

TARGET   To recall and use known ×/÷ facts.

A

What is:

1 9 × 2 18
2 4 × 7 28
3 5 × 5 25
4 7 × 11 77
5 48 ÷ 4 12
6 42 ÷ 6 7
7 18 ÷ 3 6
8 36 ÷ 12 3
9 8 × 1 8
10 12 × 10 120
11 4 × 4 16
12 6 × 8 48
13 14 ÷ 2 7
14 40 ÷ 5 8
15 63 ÷ 7 9
16 55 ÷ 11 5
17 3 × 6 18
18 5 × 9 45
19 7 × 3 21
20 4 × 12 48
21 60 ÷ 10 6
22 32 ÷ 8 4
23 5 ÷ 1 5
24 27 ÷ 9 3

B

Copy and complete.

1 [12] × 5 = 60
2 [12] × 6 = 36
3 [42] ÷ 9 = 6
4 [72] ÷ 8 = 9
5 [10] × 3 = 30
6 [8] × 12 = 96
7 [11] ÷ 10 = 110
8 [1] ÷ 11 = 11
9 [11] × 8 = 88
10 [8] × 7 = 56
11 [10] ÷ 1 = 10
12 [66] ÷ 6 = 11

Write the answer only.

13 110 × 9 990   25 450 ÷ 5 90
14 70 × 12 840   26 420 ÷ 7 60
15 80 × 2 160   27 640 ÷ 8 80
16 100 × 11 1100   28 1320 ÷ 12 110
17 120 × 6 720   29 240 ÷ 3 80
18 120 × 12 1440   30 1080 ÷ 9 120
19 90 × 4 360   31 240 ÷ 2 120
20 70 × 7 490   32 880 ÷ 11 80
21 60 × 0 0   33 540 ÷ 6 90
22 120 × 11 1320   34 280 ÷ 4 70
23 70 × 8 560   35 1080 ÷ 12 90
24 80 × 9 720   36 840 ÷ 7 120

C

Copy and complete.

1 ☐ × 7 = 770
2 ☐ × 12 = 480
3 ☐ ÷ 9 = 70
4 ☐ ÷ 8 = 120
5 ☐ × 6 = 360
6 ☐ × 9 = 1080
7 ☐ ÷ 11 = 50
8 ☐ ÷ 7 = 60
9 ☐ × 8 = 480
10 ☐ × 11 = 1320
11 ☐ ÷ 6 = 70
12 ☐ ÷ 12 = 60

Write the answer only.

13 900 × 8   25 6600 ÷ 6
14 1100 × 12   26 12 100 ÷ 11
15 1200 × 6   27 8100 ÷ 9
16 900 × 7   28 8400 ÷ 7
17 700 × 11   29 6400 ÷ 8
18 800 × 9   30 14 400 ÷ 12
19 1200 × 12   31 13 200 ÷ 11
20 700 × 8   32 5400 ÷ 9
21 1100 × 11   33 4900 ÷ 7
22 900 × 6   34 9600 ÷ 8
23 1100 × 9   35 4800 ÷ 6
24 800 × 7   36 8400 ÷ 12

TARGET To use place value and known ×/÷ facts to multiply multiples of 10/100.

Examples
$20 \times 6 = 120$ $5 \times 70 = 350$
$200 \times 6 = 1200$ $5 \times 700 = 3500$
$20 \times 60 = 1200$ $50 \times 70 = 3500$

A

Copy and complete.

1 $4 \times 2 = \boxed{}$
$40 \times 2 = \boxed{}$

2 $3 \times 5 = \boxed{}$
$30 \times 5 = \boxed{}$

3 $6 \times 3 = \boxed{}$
$6 \times 30 = \boxed{}$

4 $7 \times 4 = \boxed{}$
$7 \times 40 = \boxed{}$

Work out

5 30×3 13 5×20

6 70×2 14 8×50

7 20×8 15 9×40

8 50×4 16 4×80

9 60×5 17 2×30

10 40×4 18 8×20

11 90×3 19 6×80

12 30×8 20 5×50

21 There are 30 children in each class. How many children are there in four classes altogether?

B

Work out

1 200×4 9 50×30

2 500×6 10 20×70

3 400×7 11 80×80

4 600×2 12 30×90

5 5×800 13 80×40

6 3×900 14 40×60

7 9×500 15 70×90

8 7×600 16 60×70

17 There is 700 ml of juice in a bottle and three times as much in a jug. How much juice is in the jug?

18 Rosita saves 50p coins. How much has she saved if she has forty coins?

19 How many seconds is 90 minutes?

20 Beethoven eats 500 g of dog food every day. How much does he eat in a week?

C

Work out

1 3000×7 9 20×60

2 2000×5 10 300×40

3 5×9000 11 700×8

4 6×6000 12 90×200

5 900×80 13 7×5000

6 700×70 14 800×6

7 80×300 15 600×90

8 20×900 16 90×70

17 There are 400 passengers on a plane. Each seat costs £60. How much has the airline taken in ticket sales?

18 A factory makes 6000 clothes pegs every day. How many pegs does it make in three days?

19 Each bottle holds 900 ml of lemonade. How much lemonade is needed to fill 80 bottles? Give your answer in litres.

20 Packets of crisps weigh 40 g. What is the weight of 500 packets in kilograms?

TARGET To use place value and known ×/÷ facts to divide multiples of 10/100.

Examples   450 ÷ 9 = 50   450 ÷ 90 = 5
              4500 ÷ 9 = 500   4500 ÷ 90 = 50

A

Copy and complete.

1. 12 ÷ 4 = ☐
   120 ÷ 4 = ☐

2. 32 ÷ 8 = ☐
   320 ÷ 8 = ☐

3. 15 ÷ 3 = ☐
   150 ÷ 3 = ☐

4. 12 ÷ 2 = ☐
   120 ÷ 2 = ☐

Work out

5. 100 ÷ 5   13. 60 ÷ 2

6. 240 ÷ 4   14. 45 ÷ 5

7. 40 ÷ 2   15. 240 ÷ 3

8. 400 ÷ 8   16. 80 ÷ 4

9. 210 ÷ 3   17. 640 ÷ 8

10. 200 ÷ 5   18. 180 ÷ 2

11. 320 ÷ 4   19. 350 ÷ 5

12. 160 ÷ 8   20. 120 ÷ 3

21. One hundred and twenty books are sorted into four equal piles. How many books are there in each pile?

B

Work out

1. 8000 ÷ 2   9. 8100 ÷ 90

2. 4500 ÷ 9   10. 4000 ÷ 50

3. 1500 ÷ 5   11. 1200 ÷ 60

4. 3600 ÷ 6   12. 1800 ÷ 20

5. 600 ÷ 3   13. 1400 ÷ 70

6. 2100 ÷ 7   14. 1800 ÷ 30

7. 4800 ÷ 8   15. 4200 ÷ 60

8. 3600 ÷ 4   16. 2400 ÷ 80

17. In four weeks Louis earns £2000. How much does he earn each week?

18. There are six eggs in each box. How many boxes are needed for 1800 eggs?

19. There are 70 pills in each pot. How many pots can be filled from 6300 pills?

20. Each packet has 90 straws. How many packets can be made from 7200 straws?

C

Work out

1. 25 000 ÷ 5

2. 56 000 ÷ 7

3. 18 000 ÷ 9

4. 9000 ÷ 3

5. 54 000 ÷ 60

6. 14 000 ÷ 20

7. 16 000 ÷ 40

8. 42 000 ÷ 70

9. 24 000 ÷ 600

10. 63 000 ÷ 900

11. 30 000 ÷ 500

12. 72 000 ÷ 800

13. 12 000 ÷ 20

14. 35 000 ÷ 700

15. 28 000 ÷ 4

16. 27 000 ÷ 90

17. There are 48 000 spectators at a football match. One sixth of the crowd are children. How many children are in the crowd?

18. Each bar of chocolate weighs 80 g. How many bars can be made from 56 kg of chocolate?

19. Three hundred people attend a concert. Ticket sales total £15 000. How much does each ticket cost?

20. There are nine biscuits in each packet. How many packets can be made from 36 000 biscuits?

TARGET To multiply 2-digit numbers by one-digit numbers mentally.

Examples $46 \times 3 = 40 \times 3$ plus 6×3 $46 \times 3 = (40 \times 3) + (6 \times 3)$
                    $= 120$ plus 18 or $= 120 + 18$
                    $= 138$ $= 138$

A

Copy and complete.

1 16×2
   $= 10 \times 2$ plus 6×2
   $= \boxed{}$ plus $\boxed{}$
   $= \boxed{}$

2 23×5
   $= 20 \times 5$ plus 3×5
   $= \boxed{}$ plus $\boxed{}$
   $= \boxed{}$

3 14×3
   $= 10 \times 3$ plus $4 \times \boxed{}$
   $= \boxed{}$ plus $\boxed{}$
   $= \boxed{}$

4 31×2
   $= 30 \times \boxed{}$ plus $1 \times \boxed{}$
   $= \boxed{}$ plus $\boxed{}$
   $= \boxed{}$

5 15×5
   $= \boxed{} \times 5$ plus $\boxed{} \times 5$
   $= \boxed{}$ plus $\boxed{}$
   $= \boxed{}$

6 32×4
   $= \boxed{} \times \boxed{}$ plus $\boxed{} \times \boxed{}$
   $= \boxed{}$ plus $\boxed{}$
   $= \boxed{}$

B

Work out

1 27×2 **9** 49×5

2 55×4 **10** 35×2

3 38×5 **11** 63×3

4 13×8 **12** 24×8

5 41×3 **13** 18×3

6 26×4 **14** 44×2

7 19×2 **15** 37×4

8 52×8 **16** 56×5

17 There are 36 stamps in one book. How many stamps are there in five books?

18 Cathie's book has double the number of pages of Jessie's book. Jessie's book has 87 pages. How many pages does Cathie's book have?

19 Each packet has 8 screws. How many screws are there in 42 packets?

20 A lorry travels 59 miles on Monday and four times further on Tuesday. How far does it travel on Tuesday?

C

Work out

1 65×5 **9** 93×4

2 34×4 **10** 74×2

3 82×2 **11** 57×5

4 58×8 **12** 85×8

5 29×3 **13** 48×4

6 46×8 **14** 72×3

7 94×5 **15** 96×2

8 17×3 **16** 67×8

17 How much is sixty-four £5 notes?

18 There are 54 adults and three times as many children at a cinema. How many children are watching the film?

19 Drinks cost 79p each. What do 4 drinks cost?

20 One bar of soap weighs 95 g. What is the total weight of eight bars?

TARGET   To use partitioning to multiply 2-digit numbers by one-digit numbers mentally.

Examples $72 \times 7 = 70 \times 7$ plus 2×7 $89 \times 3 = (80 \times 3) + (9 \times 3)$
                          $= 490$ plus 14 $= 240 + 27$
                          $= 504$ $= 267$

A

Copy and complete.

1 13×4
   $= 10 \times 4$ plus 3×4
   $= \boxed{}$ plus $\boxed{}$
   $= \boxed{}$

2 25×3
   $= 20 \times 3$ plus $5 \times \boxed{}$
   $= \boxed{}$ plus $\boxed{}$
   $= \boxed{}$

3 34×5
   $= 30 \times \boxed{}$ plus $4 \times \boxed{}$
   $= \boxed{}$ plus $\boxed{}$
   $= \boxed{}$

4 18×2
   $= \boxed{} \times 2$ plus $\boxed{} \times 2$
   $= \boxed{}$ plus $\boxed{}$
   $= \boxed{}$

Work out

5 15×8 9 23×5
6 22×4 10 34×8
7 37×3 11 56×3
8 48×2 12 49×4

B

Work out

1 24×8 9 53×8
2 43×6 10 76×2
3 59×2 11 45×9
4 62×5 12 94×3

5 17×3 13 67×4
6 38×9 14 32×6
7 85×7 15 78×5
8 29×4 16 96×7

17 There are eight flowers in each bunch. How many flowers are there in 42 bunches?

18 Oranges cost 39p each. How much will five oranges cost?

19 Anika has read one third of her book. This is exactly 58 pages. How many pages are there in her book?

20 Each box holds six eggs. How many eggs are there in 26 boxes?

C

Work out

1 19×11 9 68×6
2 64×9 10 16×9
3 86×3 11 97×2
4 57×6 12 54×11

5 35×5 13 28×4
6 92×8 14 75×8
7 73×7 15 47×7
8 49×12 16 83×12

17 A water sprinkler uses 9 litres of water every minute. How much will it use in 84 minutes?

18 Cups of tea cost 99p. Arnie orders eleven teas. How much does he pay?

19 It is Petra's 72nd birthday. How many months has she been alive?

TARGET To use partitioning to divide 2-digit numbers by one-digit numbers mentally.

Examples

$78 \div 3 = 60 \div 3$ plus $18 \div 3$
$\quad\quad\quad = 20$ plus 6
$\quad\quad\quad = 26$

$85 \div 5 = (50 \div 5) + (35 \div 5)$
$\quad\quad\quad = 10 + 7$
$\quad\quad\quad = 17$

A

Copy and complete.

1. $68 \div 2$
   $= 60 \div 2$ plus $8 \div 2$
   $= \boxed{}$ plus $\boxed{}$
   $= \boxed{}$

2. $84 \div 6$
   $= 60 \div 6$ plus $24 \div 6$
   $= \boxed{}$ plus $\boxed{}$
   $= \boxed{}$

3. $95 \div 5$
   $= 50 \div 5$ plus $\boxed{} \div 5$
   $= \boxed{}$ plus $\boxed{}$
   $= \boxed{}$

4. $96 \div 4$
   $= 80 \div 4$ plus $\boxed{} \div 4$
   $= \boxed{}$ plus $\boxed{}$
   $= \boxed{}$

Work out

5. $69 \div 3$
6. $75 \div 5$
7. $44 \div 2$
8. $96 \div 8$
9. $56 \div 4$
10. $93 \div 3$
11. $86 \div 2$
12. $120 \div 5$

B

Work out

1. $92 \div 4$
2. $78 \div 6$
3. $72 \div 2$
4. $120 \div 8$
5. $210 \div 5$
6. $117 \div 9$
7. $75 \div 3$
8. $98 \div 7$
9. $96 \div 6$
10. $58 \div 2$
11. $180 \div 5$
12. $168 \div 8$
13. $56 \div 4$
14. $154 \div 7$
15. $84 \div 3$
16. $153 \div 9$

17. There are eight yogurts in each pack. How many packs can be made from 104 yogurts?

18. Three apples cost 57p altogether. What does one apple cost?

19. Each box holds seven fish. How many boxes will be needed for 126 fish?

20. Six friends share the cost of a meal. The bill comes to £102. How much should they each pay?

C

Work out

1. $198 \div 9$
2. $290 \div 5$
3. $143 \div 11$
4. $182 \div 7$
5. $168 \div 12$
6. $192 \div 6$
7. $201 \div 3$
8. $296 \div 8$
9. $130 \div 2$
10. $495 \div 11$
11. $273 \div 7$
12. $486 \div 9$
13. $324 \div 6$
14. $396 \div 12$
15. $448 \div 8$
16. $304 \div 4$

17. There are 12 inches in one foot. How many feet is 300 inches?

18. Each packet has nine crayons. How many packets can be made from 612 crayons?

19. Hannah buys six pens for £2·82 altogether. How much does each pen cost?

20. Archie realises that, as it is not a leap year, at the end of that day one fifth of the year will have passed. What is the date?

TARGET To multiply three numbers together in any order.

Examples

Multiply in any order
$(6 \times 4) \times 8 = 6 \times (4 \times 8)$
$\qquad 24 \times 8 = 6 \times 32$
$\quad 160 + 32 = 180 + 12$
$\qquad\quad 192 = 192$

Look for pairs that
make multiples of 10.
$8 \times 9 \times 5 \qquad\qquad 8 \times 9 \times 5$
$9 \times 40 \qquad$ not $\quad 72 \times 5$
$360 \qquad\qquad\qquad 350 + 10$
$\qquad\qquad\qquad\qquad 360$

Generally multiply
largest numbers first.
$4 \times (6 \times 9) \quad$ not $\quad (4 \times 6) \times 9$
$4 \times 54 \qquad\qquad 24 \times 9$
$200 + 16 \qquad\qquad 180 + 36$
$216 \qquad\qquad\qquad 216$

A

Copy and complete.

1. $3 \times 6 \times 10 = \boxed{} \times 10$
   $= \boxed{}$
2. $9 \times 4 \times 5 = 9 \times \boxed{}$
   $= \boxed{}$
3. $3 \times 9 \times 2 = \boxed{} \times 2$
   $= \boxed{}$
4. $10 \times 4 \times 7 = 10 \times \boxed{}$
   $= \boxed{}$
5. $7 \times 6 \times 5 = 7 \times \boxed{}$
   $= \boxed{}$
6. $8 \times 7 \times 2 = \boxed{} \times 2$
   $= \boxed{}$
7. $9 \times 10 \times 5 = \boxed{} \times 10$
   $= \boxed{}$
8. $4 \times 12 \times 5 = 4 \times \boxed{}$
   $= \boxed{}$
9. $6 \times 2 \times 7 = \boxed{} \times 2$
   $= \boxed{}$
10. $8 \times 10 \times 6 = 10 \times \boxed{}$
    $= \boxed{}$
11. $5 \times 3 \times 8 = 3 \times \boxed{}$
    $= \boxed{}$
12. $2 \times 11 \times 4 = 2 \times \boxed{}$
    $= \boxed{}$

B

Write answers only.

1. $11 \times 10 \times 3$
2. $5 \times 9 \times 8$
3. $9 \times 2 \times 6$
4. $8 \times 9 \times 10$
5. $12 \times 6 \times 5$
6. $3 \times 5 \times 4$
7. $4 \times 10 \times 12$
8. $2 \times 12 \times 7$
9. $7 \times 3 \times 6$
10. $20 \times 9 \times 5$

Use jottings to work out.

11. $4 \times 9 \times 4$
12. $3 \times 6 \times 12$
13. $5 \times 3 \times 16$
14. $4 \times 7 \times 8$
15. $11 \times 4 \times 12$
16. $6 \times 6 \times 6$
17. $8 \times 3 \times 11$
18. $7 \times 4 \times 6$
19. $6 \times 9 \times 11$
20. $9 \times 3 \times 7$

C

Write answers only.

1. $70 \times 20 \times 4$
2. $12 \times 7 \times 50$
3. $8 \times 9 \times 9$
4. $7 \times 11 \times 5$
5. $30 \times 8 \times 5$
6. $9 \times 3 \times 7$
7. $20 \times 4 \times 25$
8. $4 \times 6 \times 40$
9. $8 \times 20 \times 6$
10. $15 \times 3 \times 6$

Copy and complete.

11. $\boxed{} \times 3 \times 25 = 600$
12. $3 \times \boxed{} \times 7 = 126$
13. $50 \times 4 \times \boxed{} = 1800$
14. $\boxed{} \times 7 \times 8 = 224$
15. $11 \times 9 \times \boxed{} = 495$
16. $\boxed{} \times 8 \times 4 = 960$
17. $\boxed{} \times 12 \times 35 = 840$
18. $5 \times 5 \times \boxed{} = 475$
19. $\boxed{} \times 20 \times 11 = 4400$
20. $12 \times \boxed{} \times 12 = 432$

TARGET   To recognise factor pairs.

Factors are numbers that divide exactly into another number.
Factor pairs can be shown by creating arrays.

Example
Two arrays can be
made using 8 squares.

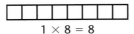

$1 \times 8 = 8$

$2 \times 4 = 8$

Factor pairs of 8: 1×8, 2×4
Factors of 8:   1, 2, 4, 8

A

1 What are the two factors of 10 shown in this array?

2 Draw a different array to show the other two factors of 10.

3 List the four factors of 10.

4 This array shows that 3 and 6 are factors of 18.

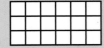

Draw two different arrays to show the other two factor pairs of 18.

5 List the six factors of 18.

6 Draw two different arrays using 6 squares. List the four factors of 6.

7 Draw three different arrays using 12 squares. List the six factors of 12.

B

1 Copy and complete this table for all numbers from 4 to 15.

Number	Number of arrays	Factors
4	2	1, 2, 4
5	1	1, 5
6	2	

2 Which two numbers in your table make a square array?

3 Can you explain why these two numbers make square arrays?

List all the factors of these numbers. The number of factors is shown in brackets.

4 20 (6) **12** 42 (8)
5 16 (5) **13** 55 (4)
6 22 (4) **14** 70 (8)
7 28 (6) **15** 100 (9)
8 35 (4) **16** 56 (8)
9 32 (6) **17** 38 (4)
10 25 (3) **18** 75 (6)
11 40 (8) **19** 84 (12)

C

1 Numbers which have a square array are called square numbers. Work out:
   a) the first 10 square numbers
   b) the 12th square number
   c) the 20th square number
   d) the 50th square number.

Find all the factors of the following numbers.

2 24 (8) **8** 21 (4)
3 45 (6) **9** 92 (6)
4 34 (4) **10** 30 (8)
5 36 (9) **11** 64 (7)
6 52 (6) **12** 112 (10)
7 99 (6) **13** 132 (12)

Fill in the box to complete each pair of factors.

14 $42 = 7 \times \boxed{}$
15 $320 = 80 \times \boxed{}$
16 $2700 = 30 \times \boxed{}$
17 $3000 = 600 \times \boxed{}$
18 $3800 = 190 \times \boxed{}$
19 $5400 = 90 \times \boxed{}$
20 $560 = 8 \times \boxed{}$
21 $600 = 150 \times \boxed{}$

TARGET   To recognise and use factor pairs in mental calculations.

Examples

$18 \times 15 = 18 \times 3 \times 5$
$ = 90 \times 3$
$ = 270$

$144 \div 16 = 144 \div 2 \div 8$
$ = 72 \div 8$
$ = 9$

$480 = \boxed{} \times 6$
$48 = 8 \times 6$
$480 = 80 \times 6$
Missing number is 80.

A

Complete the factor pairs.

1 The factor pairs of 8.
  1 and ☐   2 and ☐

2 The factor pairs of 10.
  ☐ and 2   ☐ and 10

3 The factor pairs of 21.
  21 and ☐   ☐ and 3

4 The factor pairs of 22.
  1 and ☐   ☐ and ☐

5 The factor pairs of 12.
  1 and ☐   2 and ☐
  3 and ☐

6 The factor pairs of 18.
  ☐ and ☐   ☐ and ☐
  ☐ and ☐

Find pairs of factors for each target number.

7 6 (2 pairs)

8 9 (2 pairs)

9 14 (2 pairs)

10 15 (2 pairs)

11 16 (3 pairs)

12 20 (3 pairs)

B

Find all the factors of each target number. The number of factors is shown in brackets.

1 13 (2)   7 60 (12)

2 28 (6)   8 72 (12)

3 32 (6)   9 88 (8)

4 40 (8)   10 100 (9)

5 48 (10)   11 126 (12)

6 54 (8)   12 144 (15)

Break down the second number into factors to help work out each problem.

13 18 × 6   17 84 ÷ 4

14 16 × 8   18 210 ÷ 14

15 22 × 12   19 96 ÷ 6

16 15 × 18   20 108 ÷ 12

Find a pair of factors to solve each missing number problem.

21 140 = ☐ × 20

22 270 = 9 × ☐

23 150 = 50 × ☐

24 280 = ☐ × 4

25 420 = ☐ × 60

26 320 = 4 × ☐

C

Find all the factors of:

1 66   7 143

2 96   8 135

3 114   9 156

4 150   10 131

5 128   11 196

6 121   12 180

Break the second number down into factors to help work out each problem.

13 28 × 16   17 168 ÷ 12

14 24 × 25   18 176 ÷ 22

15 22 × 18   19 165 ÷ 15

16 31 × 24   20 147 ÷ 21

Find the highest factor shared by:

21 15 and 40

22 18 and 24

23 12 and 20

24 30 and 50

25 32 and 56

26 18 and 45

27 14 and 63

28 22 and 55

29 28 and 42

30 32 and 48

TARGET   To multiply TU and HTU by U using a written method.

Examples

$$\begin{array}{r} 3\ 9 \\ \times \quad 7 \\ \hline 2\ 7\ 3 \\ {\scriptstyle 6} \end{array}$$

$9 \times 7 = 63$ Carry 60 (⁶)
$30 \times 7 = 210$
$210 + 60 = 270$

Answer *273*

$$\begin{array}{r} 3\ 2\ 9 \\ \times \quad 8 \\ \hline 2\ 6\ 3\ 2 \\ {\scriptstyle 2\ 7} \end{array}$$

$9 \times 8 = 72$ Carry 70 (⁷)
$20 \times 8 + 70 = 230$ Carry 200 (²)
$300 \times 8 + 200 = 2600$

Answer *2632*

A

Work out

1. 27×2
2. 35×4
3. 19×3
4. 5
5. 23
6. 64
7. $28 \times$
8. $36 \times$

9. 47×5
10. 56×3
11. 85×2

17. How needed 38 skie

18. Sixty-nine people pay £5 each for a coach ticket. How much do they pay altogether?

19. Pairs of socks are sold in packs of three. How many pairs are there in 47 packs?

B

Work out

1. 237×6
2. 168×5
3. 459×8
4. 158×6
5. 387×3
6. 162×8
7. 490×6
8. 354×7

9. 674×4
10. 236×7
11. 504×9

Run
s.
le
cket
sales?

18. Each sweet weighs 5 g. What do 375 sweets weigh?

19. Each row of knitting takes eight minutes. There are 147 rows in a pattern. How long will it take to knit?

20. Elsie takes four pills every day. How many does she take in a non-leap year?

C

Work out

1. 4386×2
2. 2193×9
3. 3249×6
4. 5157×8
5. 2604×7
6. 7359×5
7. 6172×6
8. 2638×9

9. 2395×7
10. 8749×3
11. 2608×8
12. 1573×6
13. 3645×9
14. 2586×4
15. 6180×7
16. 4379×8

17. A stately home has 8269 visitors, each paying £5 entrance fee. How much is taken in entrance fees?

18. The population of Westham is 5846. Three times as many people live in Eastham. What is the population of Eastham?

19. Each car weighs 1874 kg. What is the total weight of the eight cars on a transporter?

20. Aryan earns £2957 each month. How much does he earn in six months?

TARGET   To multiply TU and HTU by U using a written method.

Examples

$$
\begin{array}{r}
5\ 7 \\
\times\quad 6 \\
\hline
3\ 4\ 2 \\
\scriptstyle 4
\end{array}
$$

$7 \times 6 = 42$ Carry 40 (⁴)
$50 \times 6 = 300$
$300 + 40 = 340$

Answer *342*

$$
\begin{array}{r}
6\ 3\ 7 \\
\times\quad\ 9 \\
\hline
5\ 7\ 3\ 3 \\
\scriptstyle 3\ \ 6
\end{array}
$$

$7 \times 9 = 63$
$(30 \times 9) + 60 = 330$
$(600 \times 9) + 300 = 5700$

Answer *5733*

A

Work out

1.   64 × 2
2.   25 × 6
3.   37 × 5
4.   48 × 3
5.   52 × 7
6.   29 × 4
7.   62 × 5
8.   38 × 8
9.   59 × 2
10.   74 × 4
11.   65 × 3
12.   46 × 9

13. There is 78 litres in each bag of compost. How much is there in four bags?

14. Pens cost 49p each. Peggy buys five. How much does she pay?

15. There are eight classes in a school. Each class has 26 children. How many children are there in the school?

B

Work out

1. 386 × 4
2. 263 × 7
3. 429 × 3
4. 147 × 6
5. 738 × 3
6. 359 × 9
7. 695 × 5
8. 526 × 8
9. 307 × 3
10. 248 × 9
11. 874 × 5
12. 539 × 8
13. 576 × 2
14. 369 × 6
15. 947 × 4
16. 780 × 7

17. One jar of mayonnaise holds 325 ml. How much is there in six jars?

18. The cost of entering a half marathon is £7. 278 people take part. How much is raised by the entrance fees?

19. Each flower tray has nine plants. How many plants are there in 167 trays?

20. How much is 736 five pound notes?

C

Work out

1. 1275 × 9
2. 2568 × 6
3. 4749 × 5
4. 3674 × 8
5. 7857 × 4
6. 5438 × 7
7. 3472 × 6
8. 2789 × 3
9. 4563 × 9
10. 3856 × 5
11. 2376 × 7
12. 5239 × 8

13. There are nine nails in each pack. How many nails are there in 3908 packs?

14. A plane flies 9042 miles every day. How far does it fly in a week?

15. Tickets for an ice show cost £8. In one week 4815 tickets are sold. How much is taken at the box office?

16. Colette earns £17.59 per hour. How much does she earn in six hours?

TARGET   To develop a written method for division.

Examples

$54 \div 3$

   18     $50 \div 3 = 10$ remainder 20 (2)

3)54 $24 \div 3 = 8$

Answer *18*

$168 \div 6$

   28     $160 \div 6 = 20$ remainder 40 (4)

6)168 $48 \div 6 = 8$

Answer *28*

A

Work out

1. $45 \div 3$
2. $26 \div 2$
3. $48 \div 4$
4. $70 \div 5$
5. $32 \div 2$
6. $68 \div 4$
7. $36 \div 3$
8. $90 \div 5$
9. $56 \div 4$
10. $57 \div 3$
11. $30 \div 2$
12. $65 \div 5$
13. $42 \div 3$
14. $36 \div 2$
15. $85 \div 5$
16. $64 \div 4$
17. $38 \div 2$
18. $51 \div 3$
19. $75 \div 5$
20. $72 \div 4$

B

Work out

1. $78 \div 6$
2. $112 \div 8$
3. $75 \div 3$
4. $112 \div 7$
5. $117 \div 9$
6. $145 \div 5$
7. $108 \div 6$
8. $136 \div 8$
9. $119 \div 7$
10. $78 \div 2$
11. $144 \div 9$
12. $152 \div 8$
13. $108 \div 6$
14. $112 \div 4$
15. $162 \div 9$
16. $133 \div 7$

17. There are 126 players at a 7-a-side rugby tournament. How many teams are there?

18. There are 84 questions in a quiz. The winning team answer one sixth of the questions wrongly. How many do they get right?

19. A sprinkler uses nine litres of water every minute. How long has it been on if 153 litres have been used?

20. Cards are sold in packs of eight. Simon buys 104 cards. How many packs does he buy?

C

Work out

1. $184 \div 8$
2. $136 \div 2$
3. $261 \div 9$
4. $144 \div 6$
5. $196 \div 7$
6. $188 \div 4$
7. $225 \div 9$
8. $228 \div 6$
9. $224 \div 8$
10. $171 \div 3$
11. $245 \div 7$
12. $342 \div 9$
13. $240 \div 5$
14. $174 \div 6$
15. $288 \div 8$
16. $203 \div 7$

17. There are 156 nails in six equal size packets. How many nails are there in each packet?

18. Keisha earns £9 an hour. In one week she earns £333. How many hours has she worked?

19. A pack of eight sausages weighs 272 g. How much does each sausage weigh?

TARGET   To practise a written method for division.

Examples

126 ÷ 9

   1 4   120 ÷ 9 = 10 remainder 30(³)

9)12³6   36 ÷ 9 = 4

Answer *14*

176 ÷ 11

   1 6   170 ÷ 11 = 10 remainder 60(⁶)

11)17⁶6 66 ÷ 11 = 6

Answer *16*

A

Work out

1. 26 ÷ 2
2. 75 ÷ 5
3. 68 ÷ 4
4. 45 ÷ 3
5. 34 ÷ 2
6. 84 ÷ 6
7. 54 ÷ 3
8. 65 ÷ 5
9. 56 ÷ 4
10. 84 ÷ 7
11. 38 ÷ 2
12. 117 ÷ 9
13. 95 ÷ 5
14. 42 ÷ 3
15. 104 ÷ 8
16. 72 ÷ 4
17. 30 ÷ 2
18. 96 ÷ 6
19. 90 ÷ 5
20. 98 ÷ 7

B

Work out

1. 57 ÷ 3
2. 108 ÷ 6
3. 95 ÷ 5
4. 135 ÷ 9
5. 86 ÷ 2
6. 144 ÷ 8
7. 68 ÷ 4
8. 133 ÷ 7
9. 130 ÷ 5
10. 162 ÷ 9
11. 75 ÷ 3
12. 138 ÷ 6
13. 76 ÷ 4
14. 126 ÷ 7
15. 68 ÷ 2
16. 198 ÷ 11

17. Three pavement slabs weigh 87 kg altogether. What does one slab weigh?

18. Guy's book has 112 pages. He has read one eighth of the book. How many pages has he read?

19. Yvonne buys five theatre tickets for £80. How much does each ticket cost?

20. There are nine Penguins in each pack. How many packs can be made from 207 biscuits?

C

Work out

1. 168 ÷ 7
2. 297 ÷ 9
3. 92 ÷ 2
4. 150 ÷ 6
5. 344 ÷ 8
6. 280 ÷ 7
7. 385 ÷ 5
8. 243 ÷ 9
9. 304 ÷ 8
10. 222 ÷ 3
11. 324 ÷ 6
12. 364 ÷ 7
13. 495 ÷ 9
14. 256 ÷ 4
15. 288 ÷ 8
16. 516 ÷ 12

17. A tub holds 525 ml of ice cream. It is shared equally between seven dishes. How much is in each dish?

18. There are eight flowers in each tray. How many trays can be made from 224 flowers?

19. Tickets for a boat trip cost £9 each. Ticket sales total £414. How many tickets have been sold?

TARGET   To practise a written method for division.

Examples

$203 \div 7$

$$\begin{array}{l} \quad 2\,9 \\ 7\overline{)20^6 3} \end{array}$$ $200 \div 7 = 20$ remainder $60(^6)$

          $63 \div 7 = 9$

Answer *29*

$172 \div 4$

$$\begin{array}{l} \quad 4\,3 \\ 4\overline{)17^1 2} \end{array}$$ $170 \div 4 = 40$ remainder $10(^1)$

          $12 \div 4 = 3$

Answer *43*

A

Work out

1. $65 \div 5$
2. $96 \div 6$
3. $36 \div 2$
4. $91 \div 7$
5. $57 \div 3$
6. $153 \div 9$
7. $68 \div 4$
8. $112 \div 8$
9. $26 \div 2$
10. $126 \div 7$
11. $48 \div 3$
12. $126 \div 9$
13. $70 \div 5$
14. $136 \div 8$
15. $72 \div 4$
16. $84 \div 6$

17. A running tap loses 85 litres of water in five minutes. How much does it lose in one minute?

18. Four pencils cost 76p. How much does one pencil cost?

19. A fishmonger has 75 cod fillets. One third are on display. How many cod fillets are on display?

20. At lunchtime eight children sit at each table. How many tables are needed for 152 children?

B

Work out

1. $120 \div 8$
2. $81 \div 3$
3. $105 \div 7$
4. $171 \div 9$
5. $162 \div 6$
6. $112 \div 8$
7. $165 \div 11$
8. $153 \div 9$
9. $300 \div 12$
10. $188 \div 4$
11. $266 \div 7$
12. $225 \div 9$
13. $312 \div 8$
14. $235 \div 5$
15. $228 \div 6$
16. $182 \div 7$

17. How many 6 cm lengths can be cut from a wire 156 cm long?

18. Eight friends share the cost of a meal. The bill is £184. How much should each of the friends pay?

19. There are 238 bars of chewing gum. Altogether they equally fill seven boxes. How many bars are in each box?

20. Nine strawberries make one serving. How many servings are there in 252 strawberries?

C

Work out

1. $294 \div 7$
2. $531 \div 9$
3. $616 \div 8$
4. $264 \div 4$
5. $504 \div 6$
6. $649 \div 11$
7. $384 \div 8$
8. $804 \div 12$
9. $1232 \div 7$
10. $1538 \div 2$
11. $1242 \div 9$
12. $1014 \div 6$
13. $1592 \div 8$
14. $1148 \div 4$
15. $1092 \div 7$
16. $1476 \div 9$

17. Four identical chocolate cream eggs weigh 340 g. What does one weigh?

18. An automatic handwash uses 9 ml of liquid of soap every wash. How many washes can be made from 675 ml of soap?

19. A pie weighs 1422 g. It is cut into six equal slices. How much does each slice weigh?

20. Eight tiles have a total length of 1168 mm. What is the length of one tile in centimetres?

TARGET To practise a written method for division.

Examples

$136 \div 8$

$$\begin{array}{r} 1\ 7 \\ 8\overline{)13^56} \end{array}$$

Answer *17*

$432 \div 12$

$$\begin{array}{r} 3\ 6 \\ 12\overline{)43^72} \end{array}$$

Answer *36*

$299 \div 13$

$$\begin{array}{r} 2\ 3 \\ 13\overline{)29^39} \end{array}$$

Answer *23*

$290 \div 13 = 20$ remainder 30

$39 \div 13 = 3$

A

Work out

1 $68 \div 4$ 9 $115 \div 5$

2 $84 \div 6$ 10 $98 \div 7$

3 $95 \div 5$ 11 $78 \div 3$

4 $84 \div 7$ 12 $96 \div 6$

5 $40 \div 2$ 13 $68 \div 2$

6 $126 \div 9$ 14 $128 \div 8$

7 $51 \div 3$ 15 $96 \div 4$

8 $104 \div 8$ 16 $117 \div 9$

17 Eight train tickets cost £112. What does one cost?

18 There are 87 children in Year 5. One third come to school by bike. How many cycle to school?

19 There are 135 goals scored by teams in a football tournament. One ninth are penalties. How many penalties are scored?

20 How many full weeks are there in 112 days?

B

Work out

1 $264 \div 6$ 9 $651 \div 7$

2 $477 \div 9$ 10 $261 \div 3$

3 $354 \div 2$ 11 $693 \div 11$

4 $476 \div 7$ 12 $414 \div 9$

5 $272 \div 8$ 13 $276 \div 4$

6 $485 \div 5$ 14 $616 \div 7$

7 $738 \div 9$ 15 $462 \div 6$

8 $504 \div 12$ 16 $544 \div 8$

17 The total weight of six bags of cement is 150 kg. How much does one bag weigh?

18 Bella earns £413 in seven days. How much does she earn in one day?

19 A dripping tap loses 435 ml of water in five minutes. How much is lost every minute?

20 Each bag has eight sweets. How many bags can be made from 592 sweets?

C

Work out

1 $1401 \div 3$ 9 $182 \div 14$

2 $1192 \div 8$ 10 $195 \div 13$

3 $1158 \div 6$ 11 $204 \div 17$

4 $1692 \div 9$ 12 $336 \div 16$

5 $1390 \div 5$ 13 $308 \div 22$

6 $1043 \div 7$ 14 $400 \div 25$

7 $1776 \div 12$ 15 $442 \div 34$

8 $1384 \div 8$ 16 $726 \div 33$

17 The perimeter of a square field is 1324 m. How long is one side of the field?

18

A cyclist rides the same route every day. In two weeks he rides 378 km. How far does he ride each day?

19 There are 24 bottles in each crate. How many crates can be filled from 600 bottles?

TARGET   To use a written method to multiply and divide.

Examples

```
    2 4 8
×         7
Answer  1 7 3 6
        3 5
```

$612 \div 9$

```
      6 8
9)61⁷2
```

Answer *68*

A

Work out

1. 57×3
2. 48×5
3. 26×6
4. 63×8
5. 79×4

6. 38×7
7. 86×2
8. 45×9
9. 93×5
10. 27×8

11. $92 \div 4$
12. $108 \div 6$
13. $144 \div 9$
14. $80 \div 5$
15. $84 \div 3$

16. $120 \div 8$
17. $92 \div 2$
18. $119 \div 7$
19. $112 \div 4$
20. $117 \div 9$

B

Work out

1. 172×7
2. 358×4
3. 745×2
4. 509×8

5. 469×3
6. 628×9
7. 275×5
8. 384×6

9. $195 \div 3$
10. $456 \div 8$
11. $220 \div 5$
12. $552 \div 6$
13. $574 \div 2$
14. $342 \div 9$
15. $511 \div 7$
16. $276 \div 4$

17. One can of cat food weighs 475 g. What do eight cans weigh in kilograms?

18. There are four rolls in each packet. How many rolls are there in 296 packets?

19. Five nights at a hotel cost £345. What does one night cost?

20. Envelopes are sold in packs of nine. How many packs can be made from 756 envelopes?

C

Work out

1. 6240×4
2. 2956×7
3. 5179×6
4. 8306×3
5. 3967×5
6. 4872×8
7. 9068×2
8. 7394×9

9. $1274 \div 7$
10. $1188 \div 4$
11. $1134 \div 9$
12. $1358 \div 2$
13. $1160 \div 8$
14. $1480 \div 5$
15. $1467 \div 3$
16. $1644 \div 6$

17. A cruise holiday costs £2483 per person. What would be the total cost for a party of six people?

18. Nesta's car uses one litre of petrol every 8 miles. In one month she drives 1480 miles. How much petrol has she used?

19. Rod orders furniture for £1128. He pays one third as a deposit. How much is the deposit?

20. The Reserves are watched by 1749 spectators. Three days later seven times as many people watch the First Team play. What is the size of the crowd for the First Team game?

TARGET To use mental methods to solve word problems involving ×/÷ facts.

A

1 Divide 18 by 6.

2 Multiply 4 by 8.

3 Halve 12.

4 Find 8 lots of 10.

5 Share 15 by 3.

6 What is the product of 9 and 5?

7 Double 9.

8 How many £5 notes make £30?

9 What number, when multiplied by 4 gives an answer of 48?

10 How many days are there in three weeks?

11 What number, when divided by 4, gives an answer of 40?

12 How much is seven 5p's?

13 How many pairs can be made from 17 children?

14 There are 12 balls in each box. How many balls are there in ten boxes?

15 What is one eighth of 24?

B

1 Find 5 groups of 9.

2 What number, when multiplied by 8, gives an answer of 48?

3 What is the product of 9 and 6?

4 Divide 42 by 7.

5 Karen has two skirts and nine blouses. How many different outfits can she make?

6 How many teams of 3 can be made from 36 children?

7 There are 8 flowers in each bunch and five bunches. How many flowers are there altogether?

8 What number, when divided by 7, gives an answer of 4?

9 How many straws are needed to make seven triangles?

10 How many £10 notes make £100?

11 Eight oranges are cut into quarters. How many quarters are there?

12 What is 6 multiplied by itself?

C

1 There are 8 rolls in one packet. How many are there in 9 packets?

2 How many 20 g weights make 160 g?

3 There are eleven players in one football team. How many are there in 4 teams?

4 Find one seventh of 63?

5 A shop sells 25 flavours of ice cream in three sizes. How many different ice creams can be bought?

6 Which number, when multiplied by itself gives an answer of 121?

7 There are five cakes on each plate. How many plates are needed for 60 cakes?

8 How many seconds are there in four minutes?

9 How many weeks make 56 days?

10 How many boxes of six can be made from 58 eggs? How many eggs are left over?

11 There are 40 straws in each packet. How many packets can be made from 200 straws?

12 How many 50p coins make £3·50?

TARGET To use mental methods to solve 1-step and 2-step word problems.

Example

A shop sells 100 ice creams. $100 \div 4 = 25$
One quarter are chocolate. $100 - 25 = 75$
How many ice creams of other   Answer *75 other flavour*
flavours are sold?   *ice creams are sold.*

A

1. Neil has seventeen fish in one tank and nine in a smaller tank. How many fish does he have altogether?

2. There are 28 children in a class. 15 are boys. How many are girls?

3. Each box holds eight rubbers. How many rubbers are there in five boxes?

4. There are 20 party candles in a pack. There are equal numbers of four different colours in the pack. How many candles are there of each colour?

5. There are 24 passengers on a bus. Nine get off. Seven get on. How many passengers are on the bus?

6. Sara buys three sweets for 10p each and a toy for 50p. How much has she spent?

B

1. A book has 120 pages. Samir has read 50 pages. How many more does he still have to read?

2. There are 32 books in four equal piles. How many books are there in each pile?

3. Poppy buys one pack of 16 sausages and three packs of 8 sausages. How many sausages has she bought altogether?

4. A baker makes 60 buns. 15 are sold in the morning and 34 in the afternoon. How many buns are left?

5. Shona has 80 cm of tape. She cuts off six 5 cm lengths. How much tape is left?

6. There are 30 children in a class. Half the class are in a dance lesson. They are asked to get into groups of three. How many groups are there?

7. For lunch Abbie can choose one from each of:
   5 choices of sandwich
   4 choices of drink
   3 choices of fruit.
   How many different lunches could she have?

C

1. There are 52 cards in a pack. Half are red. How many red cards are there?

2. How many days are there in nine weeks?

3. There are 55 paint brushes in the Art Room. 19 thin brushes are kept in one pot. The rest are shared equally between three pots. How many brushes are there in each of these three pots?

4. Pencils cost 8p each. Boris buys six and pays £1. How much change does he receive?

5. In the school canteen there are 28 more children having a dinner than eating a packed lunch. 39 children are having a packed lunch. How many children are in the canteen?

6. Four tickets for a film cost £36. How much do five tickets cost?

7. Vincent has 2 suits, 5 shirts and 12 ties. How many times could he dress differently before needing to wear the same combination of suit, shirt and tie?

TARGET To use mental methods to solve 1-step and 2-step word problems.

Example

A shop has 128 pairs of shoes on display and 485 pairs in stock. How many shoes are there in the shop altogether?

```
   4 8 5                6 1 3     Answer
 + 1 2 8            ×       2     1226 shoes are
   6 1 3            1 2 2 6       in the shop
   1 1                            altogether.
```

A

1. Tickets for a boat trip cost £5 each. How much will seven tickets cost?

2. Ninety-two people work at a supermarket. 54 are men. How many women work at the store?

3. Craig has 24 sweets. He eats a quarter of them. How many does he have left?

4. There are six classes in the school. Each class has 30 children. How many children are there in the school?

5. Kim's book has 86 pages. She has read 27. How many pages does she have to read until she has read half the book?

6. Jimmy has 15p. Rashida has twice as much. How much do they have altogether?

B

1. There are nine bunches of flowers. Each bunch has eight flowers. How many flowers are there altogether?

2. A school has 225 children. 76 are out on a trip. How many children are in school?

3. Each page of Liam's exercise book has 23 lines. His story is three full pages and 17 lines long. How many lines has he written?

4. Sophie picks 174 apples. Chantal picks 38 more than Sophie. How many do they pick altogether?

5. There are 48 chocolates in a box. Half are eaten. Nine more are eaten. How many are left?

6. Pens cost 35p each. Corey buys 4 for 90p. How much has he saved?

7. Luigi makes four different pizza bases and serves 15 choices of topping. How many different pizzas does he make?

C

1. Becky saves 20p coins. She has saved £4·60. How many coins has she saved?

2. A shop has 541 pairs of shoes in stock. 179 pairs are sold. How many pairs are left?

3. One biscuit weighs 60 g. What do twelve biscuits weigh?

4. There are 27 more pupils in the Upper School than in the Lower School. There are 114 in the Upper School. How many pupils are there in the whole school?

5. Books cost £6·90. Stuart buys one and gets one half price. How much does he pay?

6. The total audience at a pantomime is 342. There are 68 more children than adults. How many adults are in the audience?

7. The menu in a restaurant lists:
   - 4 starters
   - 8 main courses
   - 6 desserts.

   How many different 3-course meals are served?

TARGET   To use mental methods to solve 2-step word problems.

Example

43 girls and 17 boys go to Gym Club. A fifth of the children are in Year 4. How many Year 4 children go to Gym Club?

43 + 17 = 60
60 ÷ 5 = 12
Answer *12 Year 4 children go to Gym Club.*

A

1. Wade is 8. In nine years he will be half the age his father is now. How old is Wade's father?

2. There are 24 marbles. A quarter are green. 8 are yellow. The rest are blue. How many blue marbles are there?

3. There are eight crayons in each small packet and twelve in each large packet. How many crayons are there in one small and 2 large packets?

4. Amy buys a box of 50 Christmas cards. She writes 26 cards. The next day she writes a quarter of the cards she has left. How many of the cards have not been used?

5. Denis has four 10p coins. He spends 7p. How much does he have left?

B

1. Eggs are sold in boxes of six or twelve. How many eggs are there in 4 large and 3 small boxes?

2. There are 83 children in Year 4. 4R has 29 pupils. 4B has 27. How many are there in 4T?

3. There are 42 women, 35 men and 17 children at a wedding. How many people are at the wedding altogether?

4. Two friends win a prize of £120. They pay the £39 bill for a celebration meal and share the rest of their winnings between them. How much do they each receive?

5. Sweets cost 9p each. Ralph buys five sweets and pays with £1. How much change does he receive?

6. Leanne has £29. She buys three cinema tickets. She has £5 left. How much does each ticket cost?

C

1. How many 20p's make the same as forty 50p's?

2. There are 547 patients in a hospital. During the following week 316 patients leave and 285 new ones arrive. How many patients are in the hospital now?

3. One fifth of the drawing pins in each packet of 80 are blue. How many blue pins are there in four packets?

4. There are 200 dogs at a show. One eighth are Jack Russells. One fifth are collies. How many of the dogs are other breeds?

5. In Assembly the children are sitting in four rows of 18 and five rows of 22. How many children are in Assembly?

6. A butcher makes 144 sausages. He makes nine packets of 8 sausages and the rest into packets of 12. How many packets of 12 does he make?

TARGET To use mental methods to solve 2-step word problems.

Example

A café has 8 cakes, each of which is cut into 12 slices. 57 slices are sold. How many slices are left?

Answer   *39 slices are left.*

$8 \times 12 = 96$
$96 - 57 = 39$

A

1. There are 100 people at a party. Half are adults. 24 are girls. How many boys are at the party?

2. A flower display is made up of 8 red, 16 yellow and 24 blue flowers. How many flowers are there in the display altogether?

3. A shop has 60 magazines. 27 are sold in the morning and 15 in the afternoon. How many magazines are left?

4. Two classes of 30 are joined together. The children get into groups of four. How many groups are there?

5. Tasha builds six squares and four triangles with straws. How many straws does she use?

6. Dirk has four packets of 20 nails. He uses 17. How many nails does he have left?

B

1. A farmer has 35 cows, 147 sheep and 16 pigs. How many animals does he have altogether?

2. A school orders 200 pencils. 168 are given out. The remaining pencils are in two equal boxes. How many pencils are there in each box?

3. A café buys five packets of 9 rolls and 17 loose rolls. How many rolls are bought altogether?

4. Rory buys two apples and a pear for 70p. The pear costs 20p. How much does each apple cost?

5. Coral has £1·63. She buys a drink for 30p and a snack for 40p. How much does she have left?

6. A carpenter has 120 screws. He uses six packets of equal size. He has 48 screws left. How many screws were in each packet?

C

1. Barry's book has 125 pages. He has read 68 pages. He reads another eighteen. How many pages does he have left?

2. Bananas are 19p. Oranges are 29p. What is the cost of five bananas and two oranges?

3. A large box has 72 biscuits. A small box has half as many. How many biscuits are there altogether in one large and one small box?

4. Train tickets cost £15 for adults. Children's tickets are half price. How much would tickets for two adults and three children cost altogether?

5. Polly has saved £28. For each of the next 8 weeks she saves the same amount. She now has £80. How much has she saved each week?

6. Wesley buys three teas for 75p each. He pays with a £5 note. How much change does he receive?

TARGET To use written methods to solve word problems.

Example

9317 people vote in an election.
The winner gets 5642 votes. How many
people vote for the other candidate?

$$\begin{array}{r} {}^{8}\cancel{9}\ {}^{12}\cancel{3}\ {}^{1}1\ 7 \\ -\ 5\ 6\ 4\ 2 \\ \hline 3\ 6\ 7\ 5 \end{array}$$

Answer *3675 people vote for the other candidate.*

A

1 Kumar has three shelves of books. There are 49 books on each shelf. How many books does he have altogether?

2 A shop has 258 customers during the morning and 192 during the afternoon. How many customers does the shop have altogether?

3 Squads of 8 players in each team take part in a netball tournament. There are 128 players at the tournament. How many teams are taking part?

4 How much is sixty-seven £5 notes?

5 Hilary has painted 546 paintings. 367 have been sold. How many have not been sold?

B

1 There are 2195 people living in a village. 1428 of them use the village shop at least once a week. How many of the people in the village do not use the shop that regularly?

2 There are seven chicken pieces in each bag. How many chicken pieces are there in 319 bags?

3 One quarter of the 268 children in a school have fair hair. How many of the children have fair hair?

4 In September 3584 students return to university to continue their studies and 1757 students begin courses. How many students are there at the university?

5 A motorway services is used by 5264 male and 4735 female travellers. How many more males than females use the services?

6 A machine makes 576 nails every hour. How many nails does it make in six hours?

C

1 In a televised talent show 93 460 people voted. The winning act received 55 784 votes. How many votes did the other acts receive altogether?

2 A store has 1428 shirts in stock. One third of the shirts are white. How many white shirts are in stock?

3 A National Park Visitor Centre has 76 927 visitors in one year. In the following year visitor numbers increase by 16 574. How many people visit the Centre in the second year?

4 There are nine plants in each tray. How many plants are there in 2435 trays?

5 A crowd of 43 157 watch a football cup tie. The crowd for the replay is 38 269. How many more people watched the first game?

6 Clothes pegs are sold in packs of 12. How many packs can be made from 1776 pegs?

TARGET   To use written methods to solve word problems.

Example

There are 228 marbles in a jar.
One sixth of the marbles are blue.
How many blue marbles are in the jar?

$$\begin{array}{r} 3\ 8 \\ 6\overline{)2\ 2\ ^4 8} \end{array}$$

Answer   *There are 38 blue marbles in the jar.*

A

1. In one year 487 boys and 469 girls are born in a hospital. How many babies are born altogether?

2. There are four cans of drink in each pack. How many packs can be made from 96 drinks?

3. A plane has 425 passengers on its flight from Manchester to Gibraltar and 179 fewer passengers on the return flight. How many passengers are on the return flight to Manchester?

4. A hotel has 75 rooms. Each room is for two people. When the hotel is full how many people are staying there?

5. A coach has travelled 376 miles. There is still 149 miles to travel. How long is the coach journey?

6. One sixth of the 84 pupils in Year 4 travel to school by bus. How many of the children come to school by bus?

B

1. Each of the nine rows in a car par has the same number of spaces. There are 441 spaces in the car park altogether. How many spaces are there in each row?

2. A school library has 2164 books. During one year 1869 have been borrowed at least once. How many books have not been borrowed?

3. Sellers pay £8 each to take part in a car boot sale. How much is raised if 193 cars are used for selling?

4. In one year 2179 caravans stopping at a site stay for more than one night while 1869 stay one night only. How many caravans stop at the site altogether?

5. Sales of programmes at a theatre raise £825. Programmes cost £3 each. How many programmes are sold?

6. Of the 7640 runners taking part in a marathon, 4375 have not run one before. How many of the runners have run a marathon before?

C

1. Harriet realises she was born exactly 1000 months ago. How old is she in years and months?

2. Marcus earns £45 317 in a year. He pays £8659 tax. How much income is left after his tax is paid?

3. Each pack has six potatoes. How many potatoes are there in 1865 packs?

4. In one year a travel company had 28 394 bookings for a river cruise and 53 768 bookings for a sea cruise. How many cruise bookings were there altogether?

5. It costs a family £1106 to rent a villa for one week. How much does the villa cost to rent for one day?

6. A driving test is taken by 62 406 people. 35 937 pass. How many people fail the test?

TARGET To solve number puzzles involving multiplication and division.

In a multiplication pyramid, pairs of numbers are multiplied together to make the number above them.

Example

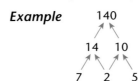

Copy and complete the multiplication pyramids.

A

1

□

□ □

6   2   3

2

□

8   □

2   □   5

3

96

12   □

□   4   □

4

32

□   4

□   2   □

5

800

□   20

□   □   4

6

320

8   □

□   □   5

B

1

□

18   30

3   □   □

2

□

21   □

7   □   2

3

4500

50   □

5   □   □

4

900

30   □

□   □   6

5

□

12   8

□   2   □

6

2400

□   30

□   □   3

C

1

□

□   □

□   □   □

3   2   5   2

2

□

□   90

10   □   15

□   □   3   □

3 Make a multiplication pyramid with three single-digit numbers on the bottom layer and a top layer of:

a) 600   c) 108

b) 180   d) 490.

1	2	3	4

4 Arrange the above numbers to form the bottom layer of a multiplication pyramid with:

a) the highest possible top layer total

b) the lowest possible top layer total.

TARGET   To solve number problems mentally.

Examples

Find three consecutive numbers with a total of 48.

Answer   *15, 16, 17*

Find two consecutive numbers with a product of 56.

Answer   *7, 8*

A

Find the pair of numbers with:

1. a sum of 18
   a difference of 2

2. a sum of 40
   a difference of 6

3. a sum of 8
   a product of 15

4. a sum of 12
   a product of 27.

Find two consecutive numbers with a sum of:

5. 11
6. 27
7. 19
8. 45.

9. I think of a number.
   I divide by 5.
   I add 9.
   The answer is 17.
   What is my number?

10. I think of a number.
    I take away 7.
    I multiply by 2.
    The answer is 38.
    What is my number?

Copy and complete.

11. $18 - 7 = \boxed{} + 3$

12. $25 - \boxed{} = 6 + 9$

B

1. Find the number.

   a 2-digit number
   a multiple of 8
   the product of its digits is 24

2. Find both numbers.

   2-digit numbers
   multiples of 6
   the sum of each number's digits is 15

Find three consecutive numbers with a total of:

3. 21
4. 36
5. 93
6. 75.

Find two consecutive numbers with a product of:

7. 12
8. 30
9. 72
10. 132.

Copy and complete.

11. $\boxed{} + 4 \times 5 = 60$

12. $32 - \boxed{} \div 3 = 9$

13. $\boxed{} + 19 - 30 = 46$

14. $9 \times \boxed{} + 9 = 108$

15. $\boxed{} \div 4 - 7 = 5$

16. $7 \times \boxed{} + 14 = 56$

C

Find the pair of numbers.

1. a sum of 100
   a difference of 12

2. a sum of 78
   a difference of 8

3. a sum of 24
   a product of 95

4. a sum of 17
   a product of 52

Find three consecutive numbers with a total of:

5. 102
6. 123
7. 177
8. 300.

Find two consecutive numbers with a product of:

9. 156
10. 240
11. 380
12. 600.

Copy and complete.

13. $\boxed{} \div 12 + 18 = 26$

14. $55 - \boxed{} \times 9 = 360$

15. $\boxed{} \div 7 - 12 = 0$

16. $\boxed{} \times 8 + 28 = 100$

17. $78 + \boxed{} \div 6 = 21$

18. $15 \times \boxed{} - 35 = 40$

TARGET To recognise and show families of equivalent fractions.

Examples

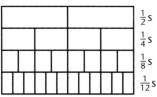

$\frac{1}{2}$s
$\frac{1}{4}$s
$\frac{1}{8}$s
$\frac{1}{12}$s

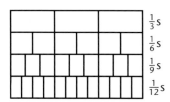

$\frac{1}{3}$s
$\frac{1}{6}$s
$\frac{1}{9}$s
$\frac{1}{12}$s

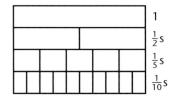

1
$\frac{1}{2}$s
$\frac{1}{5}$s
$\frac{1}{10}$s

A

Use the fraction charts. Copy and complete these equivalent fractions.

1. $\frac{3}{4} = \frac{\square}{8}$

2. $\frac{2}{3} = \frac{4}{\square}$

3. $\frac{\square}{5} = \frac{4}{10}$

4. $\frac{2}{\square} = \frac{3}{12}$

5. $\frac{6}{9} = \frac{\boxed{8}}{12}$

6. $\frac{4}{5} = \frac{8}{\boxed{10}}$

Write the equivalent fractions shown in each pair of diagrams.

7. $\frac{1}{3}$ $\frac{2}{6}$

8. $\frac{1}{2}$ $\frac{2}{4}$

9. $\frac{1}{5}$ $\frac{2}{10}$

10. 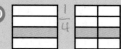 $\frac{1}{4}$ $\frac{2}{8}$

B

Use the fraction charts. Copy and complete these families of fractions.

1. $\frac{1}{2} = \frac{\boxed{2}}{4} = \frac{\boxed{4}}{8} = \frac{\boxed{8}}{16}$

2. $\frac{1}{4} = \frac{\boxed{2}}{8} = \frac{\boxed{3}}{12} = \frac{\boxed{4}}{16}$

3. $\frac{1}{5} = \frac{\boxed{2}}{10} = \frac{\boxed{3}}{15} = \frac{\boxed{4}}{20}$

4. $\frac{2}{3} = \frac{\boxed{4}}{6} = \frac{\boxed{6}}{9} = \frac{\boxed{8}}{12}$

Use the diagram to help complete the equivalent fractions.

5. $\frac{4}{5} = \frac{\boxed{8}}{10}$

6. $\frac{3}{4} = \frac{\boxed{6}}{8}$

7. $\frac{1}{3} = \frac{4}{\boxed{12}}$

8. $\frac{2}{3} = \frac{\boxed{4}}{6}$

Draw a diagram to show:

9. $\frac{3}{4} = \frac{9}{12}$ 11. $\frac{2}{5} = \frac{4}{10}$

10. $\frac{1}{2} = \frac{5}{10}$ 12. $\frac{2}{3} = \frac{6}{9}$

C

Copy and complete the equivalent fractions.

1. $\frac{4}{5} = \frac{\square}{10}$ 7. $\frac{1}{2} = \frac{8}{\square}$

2. $\frac{3}{10} = \frac{\square}{100}$ 8. $\frac{7}{10} = \frac{35}{\square}$

3. $\frac{5}{8} = \frac{\square}{16}$ 9. $\frac{5}{6} = \frac{15}{\square}$

4. $\frac{2}{3} = \frac{\square}{15}$ 10. $\frac{4}{9} = \frac{8}{\square}$

5. $\frac{3}{4} = \frac{\square}{16}$ 11. $\frac{19}{20} = \frac{95}{\square}$

6. $\frac{3}{7} = \frac{\square}{14}$ 12. $\frac{3}{4} = \frac{15}{\square}$

Continue these fraction chains for four further terms.

13. $\frac{1}{4} = \frac{2}{8} = \frac{3}{12}$ 16. $\frac{3}{10} = \frac{6}{20} = \frac{9}{30}$

14. $\frac{2}{3} = \frac{4}{6} = \frac{6}{9}$ 17. $\frac{4}{5} = \frac{8}{10} = \frac{12}{15}$

15. $\frac{5}{8} = \frac{10}{16} = \frac{15}{24}$ 18. $\frac{7}{8} = \frac{14}{16} = \frac{21}{24}$

Write three more fractions equivalent to:

19. $\frac{4}{11}$ 22. $\frac{20}{45}$ 25. $\frac{14}{18}$

20. $\frac{15}{24}$ 23. $\frac{7}{12}$ 26. $\frac{33}{60}$

21. $\frac{6}{21}$ 24. $\frac{18}{39}$ 27. $\frac{35}{42}$

TARGET   To practise counting forwards and backwards using fractions.

Example

Count on 6 steps of $\frac{1}{8}$ from 0.   0 $\frac{1}{8}$ $\frac{2}{8}$ $\frac{3}{8}$ $\frac{4}{8}$ $\frac{5}{8}$ $\frac{6}{8}$

Count back 6 steps of $\frac{1}{10}$ from 1.   1 $\frac{9}{10}$ $\frac{8}{10}$ $\frac{7}{10}$ $\frac{6}{10}$ $\frac{5}{10}$ $\frac{4}{10}$

A

Start at 0.

Copy and complete each sequence.

1 Count on 4 steps of $\frac{1}{4}$.

6 $\frac{3}{8}$ $\frac{4}{8}$ ☐   ☐ $\frac{7}{8}$ 1

2 Count on 6 steps of $\frac{1}{10}$.

7 ☐   ☐ $\frac{3}{7}$ $\frac{4}{7}$ $\frac{5}{7}$ $\frac{6}{7}$

3 Count on 3 steps of $\frac{1}{3}$.

8 0   ☐ $\frac{2}{5}$ ☐ $\frac{4}{5}$ ☐

4 Count on 4 steps of $\frac{1}{6}$.

9 $\frac{1}{6}$ $\frac{2}{6}$ ☐   ☐   ☐   1

5 Count on 5 steps of $\frac{1}{5}$.

10 ☐ $\frac{6}{10}$ ☐ $\frac{8}{10}$ ☐   1

B

Count on from 0 to 1 in steps of:

1 one third

3 one sixth

2 one tenth

4 one ninth.

Count back from 1 to 0 in steps of:

5 one quarter

7 one fifth

6 one eighth

8 one seventh.

Write each sequence.

9 Start at $\frac{3}{8}$.   Count on 5 steps of $\frac{1}{8}$.

10 Start at $\frac{5}{10}$.   Count back 3 steps of $\frac{1}{10}$.

11 Start at $\frac{17}{100}$.   Count on 6 steps of $\frac{1}{100}$.

12 Start at $\frac{8}{9}$.   Count back 4 steps of $\frac{1}{9}$.

13 Start at $\frac{5}{12}$.   Count on 7 steps of $\frac{1}{12}$.

14 Start at 1.   Count back 5 steps of $\frac{1}{100}$.

C

Start at 0.

Copy and complete each sequence.

1 Count on 4 steps of $\frac{2}{9}$.

6 $\frac{1}{3}$ $\frac{2}{3}$ 1 $1\frac{1}{3}$ ☐   ☐ $2\frac{1}{3}$

2 Count on 4 steps of $\frac{2}{7}$.

7 $\frac{1}{2}$ 1   ☐   ☐   ☐   3 $3\frac{1}{2}$

3 Count on 5 steps of $\frac{2}{10}$.

8 $\frac{3}{5}$ ☐   1   ☐ $1\frac{2}{5}$ ☐ $1\frac{4}{5}$

4 Count on 4 steps of $\frac{3}{4}$.

9 $\frac{3}{10}$ $\frac{6}{10}$ ☐ $1\frac{2}{10}$ ☐ $1\frac{8}{10}$ ☐

5 Count on 5 steps of $\frac{2}{8}$.

10 $\frac{75}{100}$ $\frac{80}{100}$ ☐ $\frac{90}{100}$ $\frac{95}{100}$ ☐   ☐

TARGET To recognise that hundredths arise when dividing one by 100 or tenths by 10 and to count up and down in hundredths.

Examples

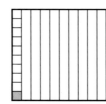

one tenth
$1 \div 10 = \frac{1}{10}$

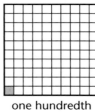

one hundredth
$1 \div 100 = \frac{1}{100}$

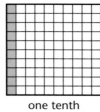

one hundredth
$\frac{1}{10} \div 10 = \frac{1}{100}$

Start at $\frac{27}{100}$.

Count on 5 hundredths.

$\frac{27}{100}$ $\frac{28}{100}$ $\frac{29}{100}$ $\frac{30}{100}$ $\frac{31}{100}$ $\frac{32}{100}$

A

Write the fraction shown:
a) in words
b) in fractions.

1   3

2   4

5 Write the fraction shown by each letter:
a) in words
b) in fractions.

6 Start at 0.
Count on 4 tenths.

7 Start at 1.
Count back 5 tenths.

8 Start at $\frac{5}{10}$.
Count on 3 tenths.

9 Start at $\frac{7}{10}$.
Count back 6 tenths.

10 Start at $\frac{2}{10}$.
Count on 8 tenths.

B

Write the fraction shown:
a) in words
b) in fractions.

1   3

2   4

Copy and complete.

5 $\frac{7}{10} = \frac{\square}{100}$

6 $\frac{2}{10} = \frac{\square}{100}$

7 $\frac{90}{100} = \frac{\square}{10}$

8 $\frac{60}{100} = \frac{\square}{10}$

9 Start at 0.
Count on 10 hundredths.

10 Start at $\frac{73}{100}$.
Count back 5 hundredths.

11 Start at $\frac{48}{100}$.
Count on 7 hundredths.

12 Start at 1.
Count back 6 hundredths.

C

Copy and complete.

1 $\frac{1}{2} = \frac{\square}{10} = \frac{\square}{100}$

2 $\frac{1}{5} = \frac{\square}{10} = \frac{\square}{100}$

3 $\frac{1}{4} = \frac{\square}{100}$

4 $\frac{4}{5} = \frac{\square}{10} = \frac{\square}{100}$

5 $\frac{3}{10} + \frac{5}{100} = \square$

6 $\frac{\square}{10} + \frac{2}{100} = \frac{62}{100}$

7 $\frac{\square}{10} + \frac{\square}{100} = \frac{19}{100}$

8 $\frac{\square}{10} + \frac{\square}{100} = \frac{84}{100}$

9 Start at $\frac{57}{100}$.
Count on 4 tenths.

10 Start at $\frac{93}{100}$.
Count back 7 tenths.

11 Start at $\frac{3}{4}$.
Count on 7 hundredths.

12 Start at $\frac{2}{10}$.
Count back 6 hundredths.

TARGET   To find fractions of numbers and quantities.

Examples

$\frac{1}{3}$ of 15 = 15 ÷ 3
    = 5

$\frac{2}{3}$ of 15 = (15 ÷ 3) × 2
    = 5 × 2
    = 10

$\frac{7}{10}$ of 60 = (60 ÷ 10) × 7
    = 6 × 7
    = 42

A

Use the array to help you find the answer.

1   $\frac{1}{3}$ of 18

2   $\frac{1}{6}$ of 18

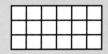

3   $\frac{1}{4}$ of 20

4   $\frac{1}{5}$ of 20

Find $\frac{1}{10}$ of:

5   40   7   60

6   100   8   90.

Find $\frac{1}{5}$ of:

9   15   11   30

10   40   12   55.

Find $\frac{1}{3}$ of:

13   12   15   15

14   24   16   36.

Find $\frac{1}{4}$ of:

17   24   19   40

18   16   20   28.

B

Find

1   $\frac{1}{3}$ of 24   9 $\frac{5}{8}$ of 16

2   $\frac{2}{3}$ of 24   10 $\frac{2}{3}$ of 30

3   $\frac{1}{4}$ of 12   11 $\frac{5}{6}$ of 24

4   $\frac{3}{4}$ of 12   12 $\frac{3}{4}$ of 36

5   $\frac{1}{5}$ of 25   13 $\frac{4}{7}$ of 35

6   $\frac{4}{5}$ of 25   14 $\frac{3}{10}$ of 70

7   $\frac{1}{10}$ of 30   15 $\frac{7}{12}$ of 36

8   $\frac{9}{10}$ of 30   16 $\frac{2}{5}$ of 45

17   There are 12 eggs in a box. Five sixths are used. How many eggs have been used?

18   An orchard has 48 trees. Three eighths are in bud. How many trees are in bud?

19   A hospital has 400 beds. Ninety-nine hundredths are occupied. How many beds are occupied?

20   There are 27 children in a class. Eight ninths are at school. How many children are at school?

C

Find

1   $\frac{5}{6}$ of 54   3 $\frac{3}{7}$ of 42

2   $\frac{7}{8}$ of 56   4 $\frac{4}{9}$ of 72

5   $\frac{7}{10}$ of 1 metre

6   $\frac{3}{5}$ of £2·00

7   $\frac{99}{100}$ of 1 kg

8   $\frac{5}{11}$ of £13·20

9   There are 80 questions in a test. Curtis answers three fifths of the questions correctly. How many does he get wrong?

10   A football match lasts for 90 minutes. The first goal is scored after five sixths of the playing time. How much time is left?

11   There are 420 g of potatoes. Two sevenths of the potatoes is removed when they are peeled. What is the weight of the peeled potatoes?

12   A coach is travelling 225 km. It stops at a service station after five ninths of the journey is completed. How much further is there to go?

TARGET To find fractions of numbers and quantities.

Examples

$\frac{1}{8}$ of 72 = 72 ÷ 8
= 9

$\frac{5}{8}$ of 72 = (72 ÷ 8) × 5
= 9 × 5
= 45

$\frac{7}{10}$ of 200 m = (200 ÷ 10) × 7
= 20 m × 7
= 140 m

A

Find one half of:

1. 22
2. 16
3. 28
4. 30
5. 14
6. 80
7. 26
8. 100.

Find one tenth of:

9. 60p
10. 20p
11. 70p
12. 40p
13. 30 cm
14. 80 cm
15. 100 cm
16. 50 cm.

Find one fifth of:

17. 20 m
18. 45 m
19. 30 m
20. 15 m
21. £40
22. £25
23. £35
24. £50.

25. Dionne has £20. She spends one quarter of her money in one shop and one fifth in another.
   a) How much does she spend in each shop?
   b) How much does she have left?

26. A doctor sees 24 people at a surgery. Half are women. One third are men. How many of the doctors' patients are children?

B

Work out

1. $\frac{1}{3}$ of 12
2. $\frac{2}{3}$ of 12
3. $\frac{1}{4}$ of 20
4. $\frac{3}{4}$ of 20
5. $\frac{1}{10}$ of 60
6. $\frac{7}{10}$ of 60
7. $\frac{1}{8}$ of 24
8. $\frac{3}{8}$ of 24

Find

9. $\frac{2}{3}$ of 18p
10. $\frac{4}{5}$ of 20p
11. $\frac{5}{6}$ of 12 m
12. $\frac{2}{9}$ of 45 m
13. $\frac{3}{4}$ of 32 kg
14. $\frac{4}{7}$ of 49 kg
15. $\frac{9}{10}$ of £100
16. $\frac{7}{8}$ of £24

Find

17. $\frac{3}{10}$ of 500 ml
18. $\frac{7}{10}$ of 20 cm
19. $\frac{11}{100}$ of 1000 g
20. $\frac{5}{100}$ of £700

21. There are 36 passengers on a bus. Four ninths are upstairs. How many passengers are:
   a) upstairs
   b) downstairs?

22. There are 30 children at a party. Two fifths drink cola. One third drink orange. How many children drink:
   a) cola
   b) orange
   c) other drinks?

C

Find

1. $\frac{3}{4}$ of £2·00
2. $\frac{5}{6}$ of £1·50
3. $\frac{2}{5}$ of £3·00
4. $\frac{2}{3}$ of £2·70
5. $\frac{3}{10}$ of 2 metres
6. $\frac{53}{100}$ of 1 metre
7. $\frac{7}{10}$ of 3 litres
8. $\frac{21}{100}$ of 5 litres
9. $\frac{9}{10}$ of £7·50
10. $\frac{2}{100}$ of £265
11. $\frac{3}{10}$ of 1·5 kg
12. $\frac{49}{100}$ of 2 kg

13. There are 48 children in Year 4. Three eighths of the children walk to school. One third come by car. The rest cycle. How many cycle to school?

14. Six sevenths of the shops in the High Street are open. Nine shops are closed. How many shops are there in the High Street?

TARGET   To find fractions of quantities.

Examples

$$\frac{5}{100} \text{ of } 600\,g = (600\,g \div 100) \times 5$$
$$= 6\,g \times 5$$
$$= 30\,g$$

$$\frac{4}{5} \text{ of } £90 = (£90 \div 5) \times 4$$
$$= £18 \times 4$$
$$= £72$$

A

Find $\frac{1}{10}$ of: Find $\frac{1}{5}$ of:

1 50   5 60
2 80   6 25
3 100 g   7 50
4 30 m   8 35

Find $\frac{1}{3}$ of: Find $\frac{1}{8}$ of:

9 30   13 32
10 21   14 56
11 £27   15 40 mm
12 18 cm   16 80 kg

17 How many minutes are there in one tenth of an hour?

18 A packet of ham weighs 200 g. One fifth is eaten. How much is left?

19 There are 100 beads on a necklace. One quarter are red. How many red beads are there?

20 There are sixty flowers in a display. One third are marigolds. How many are not marigolds?

B

Find

1 $\frac{3}{10}$ of 20 cm
2 $\frac{4}{7}$ of 14p
3 $\frac{5}{12}$ of £72
4 $\frac{7}{10}$ of 30 kg
5 $\frac{3}{8}$ of 80 g
6 $\frac{2}{3}$ of 24 litres
7 $\frac{3}{4}$ of 28p
8 $\frac{9}{100}$ of 400 ml
9 $\frac{5}{8}$ of £48
10 $\frac{4}{9}$ of 45 km

11 A roll of cling film is 24 m long. Seven eighths is used. How much is left?

12 A packet of cereal weighs 750 g. Three fifths has been used. How much has been used?

13 There are 30 safety pins in a packet. Five sixths are used. How many are left?

14 There are 180 spaces in a car park. Nine tenths are taken. How many cars are in the car park?

C

Find

1 $\frac{3}{7}$ of £49
2 $\frac{4}{5}$ of 45 m
3 $\frac{33}{100}$ of 400 ml
4 $\frac{5}{6}$ of 120 g
5 $\frac{11}{12}$ of 60 mm
6 $\frac{9}{10}$ of 160 kg
7 $\frac{2}{9}$ of 63p
8 $\frac{3}{10}$ of 1500 ml
9 $\frac{7}{8}$ of 72 cm
10 $\frac{125}{100}$ of 4000 km

11 A garden has an area of 280 m². A lawn occupies four sevenths of the garden. What is the area of the lawn?

12 A crowd of 36 000 watch a football match. Five ninths are season ticket holders. How many are not season ticket holders?

13 A bottle of washing up liquid holds one litre. One twentieth is used every day. How much is used in a week?

14 A roll of wrapping paper is 4 m long. Three fifths is used. How much is left?

TARGET To add and subtract fractions with the same denominator.

ADDING
Add the numerators (top numbers).
Denominator (bottom number) stays the same.

Example
5 eighths add 2 eighths

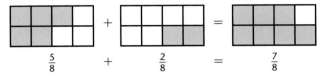

$$\frac{5}{8} \quad + \quad \frac{2}{8} \quad = \quad \frac{7}{8}$$

SUBTRACTING
Subtract the numerators.
Denominator stays the same.

Example
9 tenths take 4 tenths

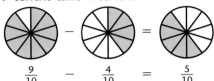

$$\frac{9}{10} \quad - \quad \frac{4}{10} \quad = \quad \frac{5}{10}$$

A
Copy and complete.

1. $\frac{1}{4} + \frac{2}{4} = \frac{\square}{4}$

2. $1 - \frac{5}{10} = \frac{\square}{10}$

3. $\frac{3}{6} + \frac{2}{6} = \frac{\square}{6}$

4. $\frac{7}{9} - \frac{4}{9} = \frac{\square}{9}$

5. $\frac{5}{12} + \frac{3}{12} = \frac{\square}{12}$

6. $\frac{8}{11} - \frac{2}{11} = \frac{\square}{11}$

7. $\frac{4}{8} + \frac{3}{8} = \frac{\square}{8}$

8. $\frac{6}{7} - \frac{2}{7} = \frac{\square}{7}$

9. $\frac{5}{9} + \frac{1}{9} = \frac{\square}{9}$

10. $\frac{4}{5} - \frac{1}{5} = \frac{\square}{5}$

11. $\frac{4}{10} + \frac{4}{10} = \frac{\square}{10}$

12. $\frac{10}{12} - \frac{6}{12} = \frac{\square}{12}$

B
Work out

1. $\frac{1}{3} + \frac{1}{3}$

2. $\frac{3}{4} - \frac{1}{4}$

3. $\frac{2}{7} + \frac{3}{7}$

4. $1 - \frac{5}{12}$

5. $\frac{2}{11} + \frac{7}{11}$

6. $\frac{7}{10} - \frac{2}{10}$

7. $\frac{8}{12} + \frac{3}{12}$

8. $\frac{6}{8} - \frac{3}{8}$

9. $\frac{2}{5} + \frac{2}{5}$

10. $1 - \frac{3}{11}$

11. $\frac{5}{9} + \frac{3}{9}$

12. $\frac{9}{12} - \frac{2}{12}$

Copy and complete.

13. $\frac{3}{10} + \frac{\square}{\square} = \frac{9}{10}$

14. $\frac{8}{9} - \frac{\square}{\square} = \frac{6}{9}$

15. $\frac{5}{11} + \frac{\square}{\square} = \frac{10}{11}$

16. $1 - \frac{\square}{\square} = \frac{3}{10}$

17. $\frac{3}{8} + \frac{\square}{\square} = \frac{7}{8}$

18. $\frac{11}{12} - \frac{\square}{\square} = \frac{4}{12}$

C
Copy and complete.

1. $\frac{5}{8} + \frac{1}{4} = \frac{5}{8} + \frac{\square}{8} = \frac{\square}{8}$

2. $\frac{1}{3} + \frac{4}{9} = \frac{\square}{9} + \frac{4}{9} = \frac{\square}{9}$

3. $\frac{1}{2} + \frac{3}{10} = \frac{\square}{\square} + \frac{3}{10} = \frac{\square}{\square}$

4. $\frac{7}{10} + \frac{1}{5} = \frac{7}{10} + \frac{\square}{\square} = \frac{\square}{\square}$

5. $\frac{9}{12} - \frac{1}{6} = \frac{9}{12} - \frac{\square}{12} = \frac{\square}{12}$

6. $\frac{2}{3} - \frac{5}{12} = \frac{\square}{12} - \frac{5}{12} = \frac{\square}{12}$

7. $\frac{4}{5} - \frac{7}{10} = \frac{\square}{\square} - \frac{7}{10} = \frac{\square}{\square}$

8. $\frac{7}{8} - \frac{1}{2} = \frac{7}{8} - \frac{\square}{\square} = \frac{\square}{\square}$

Work out

9. $\frac{1}{4} + \frac{7}{12}$

10. $\frac{2}{5} + \frac{3}{10}$

11. $\frac{1}{6} + \frac{2}{3}$

12. $\frac{4}{12} + \frac{1}{2}$

13. $\frac{5}{6} - \frac{1}{12}$

14. $\frac{1}{2} - \frac{1}{6}$

15. $\frac{3}{4} - \frac{3}{8}$

16. $\frac{7}{9} - \frac{2}{3}$

TARGET   To add and subtract fractions with the same denominator beyond one whole one.

Examples

11 eighths $= \frac{5}{8} + \frac{6}{8}$ 1 and $\frac{3}{8} = \frac{5}{8} + \frac{6}{8}$ $\frac{11}{8} = \frac{5}{8} + \frac{6}{8}$ $1\frac{3}{8} = \frac{5}{8} + \frac{6}{8}$

11 eighths $- \frac{5}{8} = \frac{6}{8}$ 1 and $\frac{3}{8} - \frac{5}{8} = \frac{6}{8}$ $\frac{11}{8} - \frac{5}{8} = \frac{6}{8}$ $1\frac{3}{8} - \frac{5}{8} = \frac{6}{8}$

A

Copy and complete.

1. one = ☐ quarters

2. one = ☐ eighths

3. one = ☐ fifths

4. one = ☐ tenths

Use the diagram to complete the pair of fractions.

5. 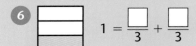 $1 = \frac{\square}{8} + \frac{\square}{8}$

6. 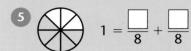 $1 = \frac{\square}{3} + \frac{\square}{3}$

7. 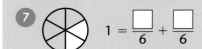 $1 = \frac{\square}{6} + \frac{\square}{6}$

8. 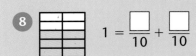 $1 = \frac{\square}{10} + \frac{\square}{10}$

Copy and complete.

9. $1 = \frac{\square}{7} + \frac{5}{7}$

10. $1 = \frac{1}{4} + \frac{\square}{4}$

11. $1 = \frac{7}{10} + \frac{\square}{10}$

12. $1 = \frac{3}{5} + \frac{\square}{5}$

B

Copy and complete.

1. 4 thirds $= \frac{2}{3} + \square$

2. 14 elevenths $= \square + \frac{5}{11}$

3. ☐ sevenths $= \frac{6}{7} + \frac{6}{7}$

4. ☐ ninths $= \frac{8}{9} + \frac{5}{9}$

5. 7 sixths $- \frac{5}{6} = \square$

6. 16 tenths $- \square = \frac{7}{10}$

7. ☐ eighths $- \frac{4}{8} = \frac{6}{8}$

8. ☐ twelfths $- \frac{9}{12} = \frac{8}{12}$

9. 1 and $\frac{1}{9} = \frac{4}{9} + \square$

10. 1 and $\frac{1}{4} = \square + \frac{2}{4}$

11. 1 and $\square = \frac{5}{6} + \frac{4}{6}$

12. 1 and $\square = \frac{3}{7} + \frac{6}{7}$

13. 1 and $\frac{2}{12} - \frac{7}{12} = \square$

14. 1 and $\frac{3}{8} - \square = \frac{6}{8}$

15. 1 and $\square - \frac{3}{5} = \frac{4}{5}$

16. 1 and $\square - \frac{8}{10} = \frac{3}{10}$

C

Copy and complete.

1. $\frac{8}{7} = \frac{6}{7} + \square$

2. $\frac{124}{100} = \square + \frac{99}{100}$

3. $\square = \frac{5}{6} + \frac{5}{6}$

4. $\square = \frac{11}{12} + \frac{5}{12}$

5. $\frac{15}{10} - \frac{9}{10} = \square$

6. $\frac{11}{9} - \square = \frac{7}{9}$

7. $\square - \frac{3}{5} = \frac{3}{5}$

8. $\square - \frac{7}{8} = \frac{6}{8}$

9. $1\frac{2}{4} = \frac{3}{4} + \square$

10. $1\frac{4}{11} = \square + \frac{7}{11}$

11. $\square = \frac{6}{9} + \frac{8}{9}$

12. $\square = \frac{67}{100} + \frac{35}{100}$

13. $1\frac{1}{8} - \frac{3}{8} = \square$

14. $1\frac{2}{10} - \square = \frac{5}{10}$

15. $\square - \frac{4}{5} = \frac{4}{5}$

16. $\square - \frac{10}{12} = \frac{9}{12}$

TARGET To recognise and write decimal equivalents of tenths.

Examples

 seven tenths

$\frac{7}{10} = 0\cdot7$

 one half

$\frac{1}{2} = \frac{5}{10} = 0\cdot5$

A

Write the shaded part of each shape as:

a) a fraction

b) a decimal fraction.

1   4

2   5

3   6

Write as decimals.

7 $\frac{8}{10}$ 11 $\frac{1}{2}$

8 $\frac{3}{10}$ 12 $\frac{7}{10}$

9 $\frac{6}{10}$ 13 $\frac{2}{10}$

10 $\frac{1}{10}$ 14 $\frac{9}{10}$

15 Write each letter as:

a) a fraction

b) a decimal fraction.

16 Write half a metre as a decimal.

B

Give the value of the underlined digit.

1 2·4   7 23·2

2 0·9   8 0·8

3 15·6   9 6·5

4 30·1   10 10·9

5 1·7   11 0·1

6 0·3   12 48·6

Give the next four terms in each sequence.

13 0·1 0·2 0·3 0·4

14 0·1 0·3 0·5 0·7

15 1·5 1·4 1·3 1·2

16 4·0 3·5 3·0 2·5

Write each letter as:

a) a fraction or mixed number

b) a decimal.

17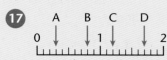

18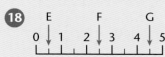

C

1 Write the shaded part of each shape as:

a) a fraction

b) a decimal fraction.

1   5

2   6

3   7

4   8

Copy and complete.

9 $\frac{8}{10} + \frac{7}{100} = \frac{\square}{100} = 0\cdot87$

10 $\frac{\square}{10} + \frac{5}{100} = \frac{25}{100} = 0\cdot25$

11 $\frac{6}{10} + \frac{\square}{100} = \frac{63}{100} = \square$

12 $\frac{7}{10} + \frac{2}{100} = \frac{\square}{100} = \square$

13 $\frac{\square}{10} + \frac{\square}{100} = \frac{49}{100} = \square$

14 $\frac{\square}{10} + \frac{\square}{100} = \frac{\square}{100} = 0\cdot16$

TARGET To recognise and write decimal equivalents of tenths and hundredths.

Examples

 six tenths
$\frac{6}{10} = 0.6$

 forty-seven hundredths
$\frac{4}{10} + \frac{7}{100} = \frac{47}{100} = 0.47$

$\frac{1}{100} = 0.01$

$\frac{3}{100} = 0.03$

$\frac{1}{4} = \frac{25}{100} = 0.25$

$\frac{1}{2} = \frac{5}{10} = 0.5$

$\frac{3}{4} = \frac{75}{100} = 0.75$

A

Write the shaded part of each shape as:

a) a fraction

b) a decimal fraction.

1 ⬡ 5 ⬡

2 ⬡ 6 ⬡

3 ⬡ 7 ⬡

4 ⬡ 8 ⬡

Copy and complete.

9 £$\frac{8}{10}$ = £ 0·8 = 80p

10 £$\frac{1}{2}$ = £ 0·5 = 50 p

11 £$\frac{2}{10}$ = £ 0·2 = 20p

12 £$\frac{9}{10}$ = £ 0·9 = 90p

13 £$\frac{6}{10}$ = £0·60 = 60 p

14 £$\frac{3}{4}$ = £ 0·75 = 75 p

B

Write the shaded part of each shape as:

a) a fraction

b) a decimal fraction.

1 ⬡ 5 ⬡

2 ⬡ 6 ⬡

3 ⬡ 7 ⬡

4 ⬡ 8 ⬡

Copy and complete.

9 $\frac{2}{10} + \frac{3}{100} = \frac{\Box}{100} = 0.23$

10 $\frac{8}{10} + \frac{\Box}{100} = \frac{85}{100} = 0.85$

11 $\frac{3}{10} + \frac{2}{100} = \frac{32}{100} = \Box$

12 $\frac{\Box}{10} + \frac{6}{100} = \frac{96}{100} = \Box$

13 $\frac{\Box}{100} = 0.09$

14 $\frac{\Box}{10} + \frac{\Box}{100} = \frac{78}{100} = \Box$

C

Give the value of the underlined digit.

1 0·5<u>3</u>   7 0·<u>8</u>1

2 0·<u>6</u>   8 0·4<u>5</u>

3 0·1<u>9</u>   9 0·<u>9</u>

4 0·<u>7</u>2   10 0·<u>2</u>4

5 0·3<u>6</u>   11 0·0<u>7</u>

6 0·0<u>8</u>   12 0·6<u>9</u>

Write as decimals.

13 $\frac{33}{100}$ 19 $\frac{17}{100}$

14 $\frac{76}{100}$ 20 $\frac{89}{100}$

15 $\frac{8}{100}$ 21 $\frac{53}{100}$

16 $\frac{92}{100}$ 22 $\frac{2}{10}$

17 $\frac{4}{10}$ 23 $\frac{5}{100}$

18 $\frac{64}{100}$ 24 $\frac{72}{100}$

Write in order, smallest first.

25 $\frac{1}{3}$,   0·13,   0·3

26 $\frac{1}{10}$,   0·9,   0·11

27 0·45,   0·5, $\frac{2}{5}$

28 0·4,   0·34, $\frac{3}{4}$

Give the answer as a decimal.

29 0·2 + $\frac{1}{2}$

30 $\frac{9}{10}$ − 0·4

31 0·55 + $\frac{17}{100}$

32 $\frac{1}{4}$ − 0·1

TARGET   To recognise, write and know the place value of decimal equivalents of tenths and hundredths.

Examples

A = 0·5   The 5 has a value of $\frac{5}{10}$.

B = 0·43   The 4 has a value of $\frac{4}{10}$.

The 3 has a value of $\frac{3}{100}$.

C = 0·57 = $\frac{5}{10} + \frac{7}{100} = \frac{57}{100}$

A

Write each of the letters as:

a) a fraction

b) a decimal fraction.

1   A   B   C
0 ────────────── 1

2   D   E   F
0 ────────────── 1

Write the shaded part of each shape as:

a) a fraction

b) a decimal.

3 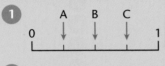   **6**

4   **7**

5   **8**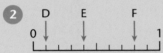

Write as decimals.

9 $\frac{4}{10}$ **13** $\frac{2}{10}$

10 $\frac{1}{2}$ **14** $\frac{9}{10}$

11 $\frac{7}{10}$ **15** $\frac{3}{4}$

12 $\frac{1}{4}$ **16** $\frac{6}{10}$

B

Write each of the letters as:

a) a fraction

b) a decimal fraction.

1   G   H   I
0.8 ────────────── 0.9

2   J   K   L   M
0.2 ───── 0.3 ───── 0.4

Give the value of the underlined digit.

3 0·4̲   **9** 0·1̲2

4 0·75̲   **10** 0·5̲

5 0·3̲9   **11** 0·0̲6

6 0·0̲3   **12** 0·2̲7

7 0·7̲   **13** 0·8̲

8 0·6̲1   **14** 0·94̲

Write as decimals.

15 $\frac{78}{100}$ **19** $\frac{29}{100}$

16 $\frac{43}{100}$ **20** $\frac{91}{100}$

17 $\frac{15}{100}$ **21** $\frac{4}{100}$

18 $\frac{6}{10}$ **22** $\frac{37}{100}$

Which is larger?

23 $\frac{1}{4}$ or 0·14   **25** $\frac{1}{2}$ or 0·3

24 $\frac{45}{100}$ or 0·5   **26** $\frac{3}{4}$ or 0·8

C

Write the decimal shown on each abacus.

1 U $\frac{1}{10}$ $\frac{1}{100}$ **3** U $\frac{1}{10}$ $\frac{1}{100}$

2 U $\frac{1}{10}$ $\frac{1}{100}$ **4** U $\frac{1}{10}$ $\frac{1}{100}$

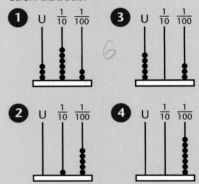

Give the value of the underlined digit.

5 8·3̲6   **11** 6̲·42

6 24·9̲   **12** 2·0̲9

7 3̲·07   **13** 5̲9·6

8 15·2̲3   **14** 33·7̲4

9 1̲·8   **15** 27·0̲8

10 7·1̲5   **16** 4·61̲

Write as decimals.

17 $3\frac{28}{100}$ **23** $8\frac{57}{100}$

18 $9\frac{1}{2}$ **24** $1\frac{3}{4}$

19 $\frac{93}{100}$ **25** $5\frac{82}{100}$

20 $2\frac{4}{10}$ **26** $3\frac{7}{10}$

21 $4\frac{6}{100}$ **27** $\frac{3}{100}$

22 $6\frac{1}{4}$ **28** $9\frac{35}{100}$

TARGET To find the effect of dividing 1- and 2-digit numbers by 10 and 100.

Dividing by 10, digits move one place to the right.
Dividing by 100, digits move two places to the right.

Examples

$8 \div 10 = 0.8 \rightarrow \frac{8}{10}$ $5 \div 100 = 0.05 \rightarrow \frac{5}{100}$

$38 \div 10 = 0.38 \rightarrow \frac{3}{10} + \frac{8}{100}$ $95 \div 100 = 0.95 \rightarrow \frac{9}{10} + \frac{5}{100}$

A

Use a calculator.
Copy and complete.

1. $47 \div 10 = \Box$
2. $2 \div 10 = \Box$
3. $55 \div 10 = \Box$
4. $9 \div 10 = \Box$

5. $69 \div 100 = \Box$
6. $4 \div 100 = \Box$
7. $52 \div 100 = \Box$
8. $90 \div 100 = \Box$

9. $73 \div \Box = 7.3$
10. $86 \div \Box = 0.86$
11. $1 \div \Box = 0.01$
12. $18 \div \Box = 1.8$

13. $38 \div \boxed{100} = 0.38$
14. $6 \div \boxed{10} = 0.6$
15. $91 \div \boxed{10} = 9.1$
16. $40 \div \boxed{10} = 0.4$

17. $\boxed{59} \div 10 = 5.9$
18. $\boxed{3} \div 10 = 0.3$
19. $\boxed{94} \div 10 = 9.4$
20. $\boxed{10} \div 100 = 0.1$
21. $\boxed{7} \div 100 = 0.07$
22. $\boxed{32} \div 100 = 0.32$

B

Do not use a calculator.
Work out

1. $57 \div 10$
2. $99 \div 10$
3. $6 \div 10$
4. $41 \div 10$
5. $4 \div 10$
6. $23 \div 10$
7. $96 \div 100$
8. $9 \div 100$
9. $87 \div 100$
10. $60 \div 100$
11. $53 \div 100$
12. $5 \div 100$

Do not use a calculator.
Work out and give the value
of each digit.

13. $35 \div 10$
14. $8 \div 10$
15. $81 \div 10$
16. $76 \div 10$
17. $3 \div 10$
18. $42 \div 10$
19. $78 \div 100$
20. $2 \div 100$
21. $25 \div 100$
22. $40 \div 100$
23. $34 \div 100$
24. $7 \div 100$

Do not use a calculator.
Copy and complete.

25. $14 \div \Box = 1.4$
26. $61 \div \Box = 0.61$
27. $\Box \div 10 = 0.8$
28. $\Box \div 100 = 0.7$

Use a calculator to check your
answers for questions 1 to 28.

C

Do not use a calculator.
Divide by 10.

1. 364
2. 12.6
3. 1607
4. 589
5. 407.2
6. 848
7. 90.5
8. 9213

Multiply by 10.

9. 0.31
10. 34.03
11. 35.6
12. 100.8
13. 9.12
14. 217.7
15. 50.4
16. 74.29

Divide by 100.

17. 5195
18. 1801
19. 567
20. 2920
21. 704
22. 4279
23. 640
24. 3068

Multiply by 100.

25. 145.1
26. 30.6
27. 2.42
28. 70.07
29. 59.3
30. 631.9
31. 2.82
32. 36.25

Copy and complete.

33. $8\,\text{mm} = \Box\,\text{cm}$
34. $71\,\text{cm} = \Box\,\text{m}$
35. $2.63\,\text{m} = \Box\,\text{cm}$
36. $4.7\,\text{cm} = \Box\,\text{mm}$

TARGET To use decimals in the contexts of money and measures.

Decimals are a way of expressing fractions. The decimal point separates the whole number from the fractions.

Examples

$\frac{1}{10} = 0.1$ $\quad\quad 1\frac{1}{2} = 1\frac{5}{10} = 1.5$

$\frac{1}{100} = 0.01$ $\quad\quad \frac{1}{4} = \frac{25}{100} = 0.25$

$2\frac{6}{10} = 2.6$ $\quad\quad \frac{3}{4} = \frac{75}{100} = 0.75$

$3\frac{17}{100} = 3.17$ $\quad\quad 9\frac{1}{4} = 9\frac{25}{100} = 9.25$

Decimals are used to show amounts of money.

Examples

1p = £0.01 $\quad\quad$ 152p = £1.52

3p = £0.03 $\quad\quad$ 415p = £4.15

80p = £0.80 $\quad\quad$ 283p = £2.83

69p = £0.69 $\quad\quad$ 626p = £6.26

Decimals are used to show metric measures.

Examples

8 mm = 0.8 cm $\quad\quad$ 1 cm = 0.01 m

25 mm = 2.5 cm $\quad\quad$ 46 cm = 0.46 m

174 mm = 17.4 cm $\quad\quad$ 130 cm = 1.3 m

50 mm = 5.0 cm $\quad\quad$ 208 cm = 2.08 m

The value of a digit depends upon its position in the number.

Examples

U	.	$\frac{1}{10}$	$\frac{1}{100}$	
£7	.	<u>9</u>	2	$£\frac{9}{10} = 90p$
£1	.	6	<u>4</u>	$£\frac{4}{100} = 4p$
0	.	<u>8</u>	7 m	$\frac{8}{10}$ m = 80 cm
3	.	1	<u>6</u> m	$\frac{6}{100}$ m = 6 cm

A

Copy and complete.

1. 10p = £$\frac{1}{10}$ = £0.10

2. 20p = £☐ = £0.20

3. ☐ = £$\frac{3}{10}$ = £☐

4. ☐ = £$\frac{4}{10}$ = £☐

5. 50p = £☐ = £0.50

6. 60p = £$\frac{6}{10}$= £☐

7. ☐ = £☐ = £0.70

8. 80p = £$\frac{8}{10}$ = £☐

9. 90p = £☐ = £☐

10. ☐ = £☐ = £1.00

Change these amounts to pounds and pence.

11. 148p

12. 32p

13. 709p

14. 465p

15. 683p

16. 257p

17. 91p

18. 508p

Change these measurements to centimetres.

19. 35 mm

20. 4 mm

21. 41 mm

22. 107 mm

23. 2 mm

24. 129 mm

25. 93 mm

26. 8 mm

Change these measurements to metres.

27. 70 cm

28. 226 cm

29. 91 cm

30. 508 cm

31. 143 cm

32. 32 cm

33. 709 cm

34. 465 cm

B

Write the measurements shown by the arrows in:

a) centimetres   b) metres.

Give the value of the underlined figure in each of these numbers.

7 £5·4<u>2</u>
8 £13·<u>8</u>0
9 £<u>2</u>7·65
10 £0·9<u>2</u>
11 £<u>8</u>·04
12 £16·<u>1</u>7

13 2·<u>9</u> m
14 0·5<u>2</u> m
15 1<u>5</u>·3 m
16 <u>3</u>0·48 m
17 6·<u>7</u>1 m
18 2<u>1</u>·07 m

Give the next four terms in each of these sequences.

19 £0·10   £0·20   £0·30   £0·40
20 0·1 m   0·3 m   0·5 m   0·7 m
21 £0·20   £0·40   £0·60   £0·80
22 0·05 m   0·1 m   0·15 m   0·2 m
23 £0·04   £0·08   £0·12   £0·16
24 0·5 m   1·0 m   1·5 m   2·0 m

Write the answers only.

25 0·2 m + 0·3 m
26 0·5 m + 0·4 m
27 1·3 m + 0·3 m
28 1·1 m + 0·5 m

29 0·8 m − 0·6 m
30 0·9 m − 0·4 m
31 1·6 m − 0·3 m
32 1·7 m − 0·6 m

33 £0·30 + £0·40
34 £0·60 + £0·25
35 £1·20 + £0·50
36 £1·40 + £0·45

37 £0·70 − £0·10
38 £0·80 − £0·15
39 £1·50 − £0·40
40 £1·95 − £0·70

C

1 Write the measurement shown by each letter as:

a) kilometres   b) metres.

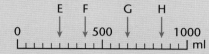

2 Write the measurement shown by each letter as:

a) millilitres   b) litres.

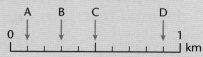

3 Write the measurement shown by each letter as:

a) grams   b) kilograms.

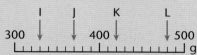

Give the value of the red digit.

4 3·15 km
5 0·62 km
6 15·9 km
7 0·07 km
8 7·5 litres
9 29·04 litres

10 60·4 litres
11 71·89 litres
12 4·03 kg
13 0·28 kg
14 52·8 kg
15 8·76 kg

Copy and complete.

16 1860 m = ☐ km
17 92 300 m = ☐ km
18 240 g = ☐ kg
19 7500 g = ☐ kg
20 60 190 ml = ☐ litres
21 700 ml = ☐ litres

22 4·31 km = ☐ m
23 0·97 km = ☐ m
24 18·4 kg = ☐ g
25 0·6 kg = ☐ g
26 36·05 litres = ☐ ml
27 2·8 litres = ☐ ml

TARGET To practise counting forwards and backwards using decimal fractions.

Examples

Count on 6 steps of $\frac{1}{100}$ from 0·27. 0·27 0·28 0·29 0·3 0·31 0·32 0·33

Count back 6 steps of $\frac{1}{10}$ from 1·45. 1·45 1·35 1·25 1·15 1·05 0·95 0·85

A

Write out each sequence.

1 Start at 0. Count on 5 tenths.

2 Start at 0·4. Count on 6 tenths.

3 Start at 2·3. Count on 4 tenths.

4 Start at 3·8. Count on 5 tenths.

5 Start at 1. Count on 6 tenths.

6 Start at 5·6. Count on 7 tenths.

Write out each sequence.

7 Start at 1. Count back 5 tenths.

8 Start at 3·7. Count back 6 tenths.

9 Start at 5. Count back 4 tenths.

10 Start at 2·4. Count back 7 tenths.

11 Start at 10. Count back 4 tenths.

12 Start at 5·1. Count back 6 tenths.

B

Write out each sequence. Count on:

1 five hundredths from 0

2 six tenths from 0·79

3 eight hundredths from 0·62

4 five tenths from 0·14

5 four hundredths from 0·5

6 seven hundredths from 1·35

Write out each sequence. Count back:

7 seven tenths from 5·43

8 five hundredths from 0·72

9 six hundredths from 1

10 three tenths from 2·25

11 nine hundredths from 2·13

12 four hundredths from 0·9

C

Complete each sequence.

1 0·5 ☐ ☐ ☐ 2·5 3

2 1·8 1·85 1·9 ☐ ☐ ☐

3 2·62 ☐ 2·66 ☐ 2·7 ☐

4 ☐ 0·5 ☐ 1 ☐ 1·5

5 4·65 ☐ ☐ 4·95 ☐ 5·15

6 ☐ ☐ ☐ 5·64 6·64 7·64

Write the first six numbers in each sequence.

7 Start at 3·3. Count back in steps of 0·2.

8 Start at 0·72. Count on in steps of 0·09.

9 Start at 5·1. Count back in steps of 0·04.

10 Start at 0·4. Count on in steps of 0·15.

11 Start at 1·81. Count back in steps of 0·3.

12 Start at 2·18. Count on in steps of 0·06.

TARGET To round decimals with one decimal place to the nearest whole number.

To round a decimal fraction to the nearest whole number look at the tenths column.
If the number in the tenths column is less than 5, round down.
If the number in the tenths column is 5 or more than 5, round up.

Examples

8·7 rounds to 9	£2·60 rounds to £3	8·3 m rounds to 8 m
16·2 rounds to 16	£4·90 rounds to £5	7·5 m rounds to 8 m
0·54 rounds to 1	£9·37 rounds to £9	12·81 m rounds to 13 m

A

Round to the nearest:

10 **100**

1 73
2 29
3 62
4 37
5 84
6 257
7 649
8 726
9 483
10 514

10 **100**

11 546
12 491
13 118
14 875
15 253
16 1170
17 2832
18 9460
19 3191
20 7905

Approximate by rounding to the nearest 10.

21 37 + 82
22 74 + 55
23 93 − 46
24 127 − 68
25 19 × 8
26 48 × 4
27 32 × 5
28 86 × 3

B

Round to the nearest whole one.

1 5·3
2 12·9
3 9·1
4 7·5
5 34·7
6 18·2
7 28·8
8 3·6
9 151·4
10 99·9

Round to the nearest pound.

11 £2·80
12 £18·30
13 £54·50
14 £9·70
15 £73·20
16 £36·10
17 £124·90
18 £81·60
19 £165·40
20 £47·80

Approximate by rounding to the nearest whole one.

21 24·3 + 8·5
22 36·4 + 29·7
23 17·9 − 5·6
24 65·2 − 37·4
25 6·8 × 9·1
26 12·7 × 6·2
27 31·6 ÷ 4·1
28 53·52 ÷ 8·9

C

Round to the nearest:
a) whole one b) tenth.

1 3·57
2 9·29
3 17·45
4 20·83
5 4·68
6 85·92
7 138·31
8 10·74
9 92·15
10 326·56

Round to the nearest:
a) metre b) 10 cm.

11 4·36 m
12 6·51 m
13 9·09 m
14 13·27 m
15 5·62 m
16 33·88 m
17 7·13 m
18 18·95 m
19 22·48 m
20 49·74 m

Approximate by rounding to the nearest whole one.

21 78·61 + 38·27
22 95·16 + 44·64
23 103·73 − 68·52
24 267·39 − 29·45
25 12·92 × 5·28
26 8·07 × 8·73
27 139·54 ÷ 19·82
28 63·71 ÷ 8·09

TARGET   To compare and order decimals.

Examples

Arrange these decimals in order, smallest first.

Look at the highest value digits first.
If these are the same look at the next highest.

The correct order is   0·35,   0·36,   0·56,   0·63

$$0.63 \quad 0.35 \quad 0.36 \quad 0.56$$
$$\frac{6}{10} \quad\quad \frac{3}{10} \quad\quad \frac{3}{10} \quad\quad \frac{5}{10}$$
$$\uparrow \quad\quad \uparrow \quad\quad \uparrow \quad\quad \uparrow$$
$$0.63 \quad 0.35 \quad 0.36 \quad 0.56$$
$$\downarrow \quad\quad \downarrow$$
$$\frac{5}{100} \quad\quad \frac{6}{100}$$

A

Write the larger of each pair of decimals.

1. 14   1·4
2. 5·2   25
3. 3·6   6·0
4. 9·0   0·9
5. 2·0   2·2

6. 17   7·0
7. 4·0   3·4
8. 6·7   7·6
9. 4·8   8·1
10. 5·3   3·5

11. Copy the number line. Put each number from the box on the line.

| 1·1   0·4   1·9   1·0   0·7   1·3 |

0 ⌞ı ı ı ı ı ı ı ı ı ı ı ı ı ı ı ı ı ı ı ı⌟ 2

B

Write the larger of each pair of decimals.

1. 5·42   5·27
2. 1·18   0·81
3. 1·35   1·53
4. 1·09   0·99

5. 4·06   4·13
6. 12·19   11·92
7. 0·87   1·05
8. 2·55   2·49

Arrange these decimals in order.
Write the smallest first.

9. 4·0,   4·4,   3·3,   3·4,   4·3
10. 2·15,   1·22,   1·52,   2·51,   1·25
11. 6·69,   9·06,   9·09,   6·66,   6·99
12. 8·17,   7·88,   7·78,   8·07,   7·77

13. Copy the line and locate the numbers.

| 1·09   0·97   1·03   0·92   1·0   1·05 |

0·9 ⌞ı ı ı ı ı ı ı ı ı ı ı ı ı ı ı ı ı ı ı ı⌟ 1·1

C

Arrange these decimals in order.
Write the smallest first.

1. 6·6,   6·02,   6·26,   2·66,   6·2
2. 5·08,   5·8,   0·85,   5·5,   5·55
3. 1·11,   1·01,   1·1,   1·4,   1·04
4. 3·7,   3·07,   3·71,   3·17,   0·73

What number lies half way between:

5. 2 and 3
6. 1 and 4
7. 5 and 5·4
8. 7·0 and 7·1

9. 3·5 and 4
10. 6·9 and 7·3
11. 9·9 and 10
12. 0·7 and 2?

13. Draw a number line from 0·9 to 1·0 with 20 divisions. Put these numbers on your line.

| 0·95   0·98   0·915   0·995   0·93   0·965 |

TARGET To locate decimals on a number line.

A

Write each number shown by the letters as a decimal fraction.

1
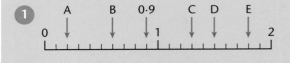

2
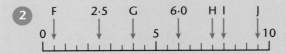

Copy the line and locate the numbers.

3
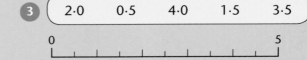

4

B

Write each number shown by the letters as a decimal fraction.

1
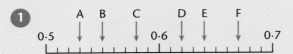

2
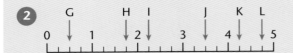

3
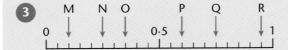

4
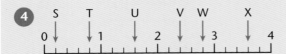

Copy the line and locate the numbers.

5
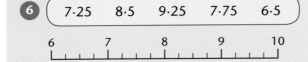

6

C

Write each number shown by the letters as a decimal fraction.

1
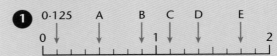

2
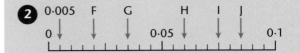

3
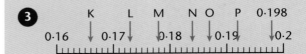

4
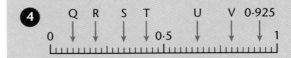

Copy the line and locate the numbers.

5
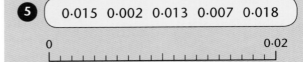

6
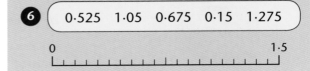

TARGET   To convert between metric units of length.

Examples

10 mm = 1 cm	100 cm = 1 m	1000 m = 1 km
54 mm = 5·4 cm	350 cm = 3·5 m	200 m = 0·2 km
7 mm = 0·7 cm	470 cm = 4·7 m	6100 m = 6·1 km

A

Copy and complete.

1. 30 mm = ☐ cm
2. 75 mm = ☐ cm
3. 4 cm = ☐ mm
4. 1·5 cm = ☐ mm

5. 200 cm = ☐ m
6. 850 cm = ☐ m
7. 5 m = ☐ cm
8. 9·5 m = ☐ cm

9. 6000 m = ☐ km
10. 3500 m = ☐ km
11. 7 km = ☐ m
12. 4·5 km = ☐ m

Which metric unit would you use to measure:

13. the length of a newspaper
14. the height of a lamp post
15. the length of a bus route
16. the width of a ruler.

B

Copy and complete.

1. 62 mm = ☐ cm
2. 24 mm = ☐ cm
3. 0·7 cm = ☐ mm
4. 9·3 cm = ☐ mm

5. 490 cm = ☐ m
6. 160 cm = ☐ m
7. 7·8 m = ☐ cm
8. 3·1 m = ☐ cm

9. 5700 m = ☐ km
10. 400 m = ☐ km
11. 8·2 km = ☐ m
12. 2·9 km = ☐ m

Think of three things with a length of about:

13. 0·08 m
14. 20 mm
15. 0·05 km

16. Estimate the length of your pencil.
    Write your estimate:
    a) in millimetres
    b) in centimetres.
    Measure the actual length.

C

Copy and complete.

1. 542 cm = ☐ m
2. 36 cm = ☐ m
3. 805 cm = ☐ m
4. 3·59 m = ☐ cm
5. 6·74 m = ☐ cm
6. 2·18 m = ☐ cm

7. 5250 m = ☐ km
8. 610 m = ☐ km
9. 1070 m = ☐ km
10. 9·83 km = ☐ m
11. 0·95 km = ☐ m
12. 7·34 km = ☐ m

Copy and complete each sentence by choosing the best estimate.

13. A television is (0·08 m, 800 cm, 800 mm) wide.
14. A room has a height of (2·7 m, 270 mm, 720 cm).
15. A vase is (2 cm, 250 mm, 0·05 m) tall.
16. A rubber has a length of (0·45 m, 4·5 mm, 4·5 cm).

TARGET To convert between grams and kilograms.

Examples

1000 g = 1 kg	500 g = 0·5 kg	2400 g = 2·4 kg
4000 g = 4 kg	7500 g = 7·5 kg	8700 g = 8·7 kg

A

Copy and complete.

1. 5000 g = ☐ kg
2. 2000 g = ☐ kg
3. 7000 g = ☐ kg
4. 3 kg = ☐ g
5. 6 kg = ☐ g
6. 1 kg = ☐ g
7. 4500 g = ☐ kg
8. 1500 g = ☐ kg
9. 8500 g = ☐ kg
10. 2·5 kg = ☐ g
11. 9·5 kg = ☐ g
12. 3·5 kg = ☐ g

Which metric unit would you use to measure the weight of:

13. a phone
14. a cat
15. a cushion
16. a baby.

B

Copy and complete.

1. 4200 g = ☐ kg
2. 1900 g = ☐ kg
3. 7300 g = ☐ kg
4. 3·1 kg = ☐ g
5. 0·4 kg = ☐ g
6. 6·8 kg = ☐ g
7. 2600 g = ☐ kg
8. 700 g = ☐ kg
9. 9200 g = ☐ kg
10. 5·3 kg = ☐ g
11. 8·1 kg = ☐ g
12. 4·6 kg = ☐ g

Think of three things with a weight of about:

13. 1500 grams
14. 0·7 kilograms
15. 250 grams.

16. Estimate the weight of a reading book.
    Write your estimate:
    a) in grams
    b) in kilograms.

    Measure the actual weight of your book.

C

Copy and complete.

1. 2940 g = ☐ kg
2. 8820 g = ☐ kg
3. 670 g = ☐ kg
4. 1·05 kg = ☐ g
5. 4·78 kg = ☐ g
6. 9·13 kg = ☐ g
7. 6290 g = ☐ kg
8. 3960 g = ☐ kg
9. 5610 g = ☐ kg
10. 2·45 kg = ☐ g
11. 0·86 kg = ☐ g
12. 7·18 kg = ☐ g

Copy and complete each sentence by choosing the best estimate.

13. A bar of soap weighs (1 kg, 0·01 kg, 100 g).

14. Each sandwich was made using (0·02 kg, 2 g, 0·2 kg) of cheese.

15. A brick weighs (8 g, 0·08 kg, 0·8 kg).

TARGET   To convert between millilitres and litres.

Examples

1000 ml = 1 litre   1500 ml = 1·5 litres   6200 ml = 6·2 litres

3000 ml = 3 litres   8500 ml = 8·5 litres   900 ml = 0·9 litres

A

Copy and complete.

1.   4000 ml = ☐ litres
2.   2000 ml = ☐ litres
3.   5000 ml = ☐ litres

4.   1 litre = ☐ ml
5.   9 litres = ☐ ml
6.   6 litres = ☐ ml

7.   3500 ml = ☐ litres
8.   8500 ml = ☐ litres
9.   500 ml = ☐ litres

10.   4·5 litres = ☐ ml
11.   2·5 litres = ☐ ml
12.   7·5 litres = ☐ ml

Which metric unit would you use to measure the capacity of:

13. a glass
14. a washing up bowl
15. a cereal bowl
16. a bucket.

B

Copy and complete.

1.   3200 ml = ☐ litres
2.   6400 ml = ☐ litres
3.   700 ml = ☐ litres

4.   2·9 litres = ☐ ml
5.   8·3 litres = ☐ ml
6.   4·1 litres = ☐ ml

7.   7600 ml = ☐ litres
8.   1200 ml = ☐ litres
9.   5700 ml = ☐ litres

10.   3·8 litres = ☐ ml
11.   0·3 litres = ☐ ml
12.   9·4 litres = ☐ ml

Think of three things with a capacity of about:

13. 0·1 litres
14. 2000 ml
15. 0·5 litres

Estimate the capacity of a water pot used for painting lessons. Write your estimate:

a) in millilitres

b) in litres.

Measure the actual capacity of the pot.

C

Copy and complete.

1.   2630 ml = ☐ litres
2.   9580 ml = ☐ litres
3.   1840 ml = ☐ litres

4.   5·05 litres = ☐ ml
5.   0·47 litres = ☐ ml
6.   3·71 litres = ☐ ml

7.   4960 ml = ☐ litres
8.   6120 ml = ☐ litres
9.   650 ml = ☐ litres

10.   7·09 litres = ☐ ml
11.   2·53 litres = ☐ ml
12.   8·27 litres = ☐ ml

Copy and complete each sentence by choosing the best estimate.

13. A can of drink holds (0·05 litres, 35 ml, 0·35 litres).

14. A tea cup has a capacity of (0·2 litres, 2 litres, 20 ml).

15. A tablespoon has a capacity of (1 ml, 0·01 litres, 100 ml).

TARGET To convert between metric units of length.

Examples

50 mm = 5 cm	490 cm = 4·9 m	1700 m = 1·7 km
126 mm = 12·6 cm	30 cm = 0·3 m	230 m = 0·23 km
8 mm = 0·8 cm	278 cm = 2·78 m	3050 m = 3·05 km

A

Copy and complete.

1. 24 mm = ☐ cm

2. 3 mm = ☐ cm

3. 9·6 cm = ☐ mm

4. 3·1 cm = ☐ mm

5. 880 cm = ☐ m

6. 590 cm = ☐ m

7. 0·7 m = ☐ cm

8. 4·6 m = ☐ cm

9. 7300 m = ☐ km

10. 400 m = ☐ km

11. 1·2 km = ☐ m

12. 6·1 km = ☐ m

13. A pile of eight identical books is 24 cm tall. How wide is each book in millimetres?

14. A reel of tape is 5 m long. 40 cm is used. How much tape is left?

B

Copy and complete.

1. 66 mm = ☐ cm

2. 185 mm = ☐ cm

3. 1·3 cm = ☐ mm

4. 14·4 cm = ☐ mm

5. 157 cm = ☐ m

6. 81 cm = ☐ m

7. 7·62 m = ☐ cm

8. 2·09 m = ☐ cm

9. 5340 m = ☐ km

10. 3720 m = ☐ km

11. 9·95 km = ☐ m

12. 0·58 km = ☐ m

13. Each length of a model railway track is 30 cm long. How long are twelve lengths of track in metres?

14. Arlene's finger is 8·3 cm long. Chandra's is 9 mm shorter. How long is Chandra's finger?

C

Copy and complete.

1. 4916 mm = ☐ m

2. 582 mm = ☐ m

3. 1·704 m = ☐ mm

4. 0·09 m = ☐ mm

5. 1215 cm = ☐ m

6. 0·5 cm = ☐ m

7. 6·08 m = ☐ cm

8. 13·9 m = ☐ cm

9. 827 m = ☐ km

10. 24 m = ☐ km

11. 5·096 km = ☐ m

12. 0·003 km = ☐ m

13. Omar's journey to school is 1·64 km. Tudor's journey is 575 m further. How long is Tudor's journey to school?

14. A row of twenty carpet tiles is 9 m long. How long is one tile in centimetres?

TARGET   To convert between grams and kilograms.

Examples

4000 g = 4 kg	2300 g = 2·3 kg	1460 g = 1·46 kg
7500 g = 7·5 kg	9800 g = 9·8 kg	3710 g = 3·71 kg

A

Copy and complete.

1. 4300 g = ☐ kg
2. 6900 g = ☐ kg
3. 800 g = ☐ kg

4. 8·2 kg = ☐ g
5. 2·7 kg = ☐ g
6. 5·1 kg = ☐ g

7. 3600 g = ☐ kg
8. 1400 g = ☐ kg
9. 9300 g = ☐ kg

10. 7·8 kg = ☐ g
11. 0·2 kg = ☐ g
12. 4·9 kg = ☐ g

13. Ten identical apples have a total weight of 1·5 kg. What does one apple weigh in grams?

B

Copy and complete.

1. 5620 g = ☐ kg
2. 1190 g = ☐ kg
3. 8740 g = ☐ kg

4. 3·05 kg = ☐ g
5. 0·57 kg = ☐ g
6. 7·41 kg = ☐ g

7. 4230 g = ☐ kg
8. 6350 g = ☐ kg
9. 760 g = ☐ kg

10. 2·97 kg = ☐ g
11. 9·53 kg = ☐ g
12. 1·85 kg = ☐ g

13. A bag of chips weighs 2·5 kg. 850 g is used. How much is left?

14. Each pepper pot holds 80 g. How much pepper is needed to fill 30 pots? Give your answer in kilograms.

C

Copy and complete.

1. 2659 g = ☐ kg
2. 7305 g = ☐ kg
3. 3192 g = ☐ kg

4. 1·574 kg = ☐ g
5. 0·908 kg = ☐ g
6. 9·745 kg = ☐ g

7. 5261 g = ☐ kg
8. 827 g = ☐ kg
9. 10 853 g = ☐ kg

10. 1·485 kg = ☐ g
11. 6·916 kg = ☐ g
12. 15·32 kg = ☐ g

13. One can of fruit cocktail weighs 400 g. What do 60 cans weigh in kilograms?

14. Benita weighs 32·45 kg. Harley weighs 900 g more. What does Harley weigh?

TARGET To convert between millilitres and litres.

Examples

8000 ml = 8 litres   100 ml = 0·1 litres   1930 ml = 1·93 litres

2500 ml = 2·5 litres   5800 ml = 5·8 litres   7260 ml = 7·26 litres

A

Copy and complete.

1. 7200 ml = ☐ litres
2. 900 ml = ☐ litres
3. 4700 ml = ☐ litres

4. 2·1 litres = ☐ ml
5. 5·4 litres = ☐ ml
6. 3·8 litres = ☐ ml

7. 1300 ml = ☐ litres
8. 8900 ml = ☐ litres
9. 2600 ml = ☐ litres

10. 9·2 litres = ☐ ml
11. 0·3 litres = ☐ ml
12. 6·7 litres = ☐ ml

13. A can of paint holds 2 litres. 400 ml is used. How much paint is left?

14. Each glass has a capacity of 200 ml. What is the total capacity of ten glasses in litres?

B

Copy and complete.

1. 2820 ml = ☐ litres
2. 6070 ml = ☐ litres
3. 1750 ml = ☐ litres

4. 8·31 litres = ☐ ml
5. 0·49 litres = ☐ ml
6. 4·13 litres = ☐ ml

7. 3280 ml = ☐ litres
8. 7540 ml = ☐ litres
9. 650 ml = ☐ litres

10. 2·36 litres = ☐ ml
11. 5·71 litres = ☐ ml
12. 9·05 litres = ☐ ml

13. Bryn makes a drink by mixing 1·8 litres of water and 450 ml of juice. How much drink has he made?

14. A dripping tap loses 3 litres of water in one hour. How much water is lost every minute? Give your answer in millilitres.

C

Copy and complete.

1. 3264 ml = ☐ litres
2. 891 ml = ☐ litres
3. 8505 ml = ☐ litres

4. 4·352 litres = ☐ ml
5. 1·478 litres = ☐ ml
6. 7·925 litres = ☐ ml

7. 2716 ml = ☐ litres
8. 9033 ml = ☐ litres
9. 659 ml = ☐ litres

10. 5·581 litres = ☐ ml
11. 0·425 litres = ☐ ml
12. 3·74 litres = ☐ ml

13. One serving of soup is 300 ml. How much soup is needed for 70 servings? Give your answer in litres.

14. A fish tank holds 28·67 litres of water. A further 1275 ml is added. How much water is in the tank?

TARGET To measure weight and convert between grams and kilograms.

A

Write the measurement shown by each arrow.

1 kg 0 1 2 3 4

2 g 60 70 80 90 100

3 kg 0 5 10

4 g 0 50 100

5 kg 0 2 4

6 g 0 50 100 150 200

7 kg 10 15 20 25 30

8 g 400 450 500 550 600

9 g 200 400 600

10 kg 25 30 35

B

Write the measurement shown by each arrow as:

a) grams   **b)** kilograms.

1 kg 0 4 8

2 g 0 200 400

3 kg 0 0.5 1

4 g 0 250 500

5 kg 0 0.25 0.5 0.75 1

6 g 0 200 400

7 g 700 800

8 kg 30 40

9 kg 2 3

10 g 500 600 700

C

Write the measurement shown by each arrow as:

a) grams   **b)** kilograms.

1 kg 0 1

2 kg 0 4 8

3 kg 0 0.1

4 g 0 250

5 kg 0 4

6 g 0 500

7 kg 8 9

8 g 500 550

9 kg 5 6

10 g 200 225 250

TARGET   To measure capacity and convert between litres and millilitres.

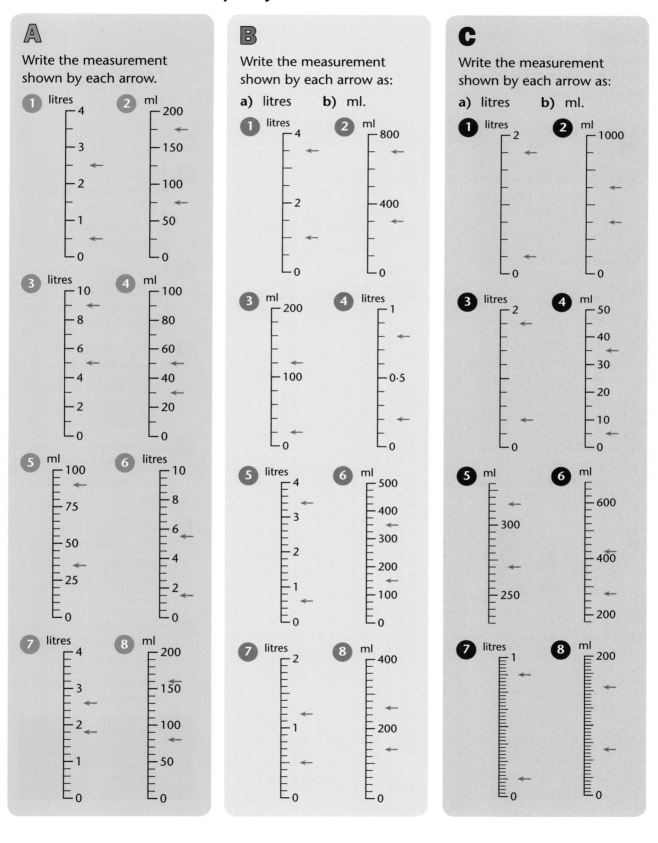

A

Write the measurement shown by each arrow.

B

Write the measurement shown by each arrow as:

a) litres   b) ml.

C

Write the measurement shown by each arrow as:

a) litres   b) ml.

TARGET To solve word problems involving the conversion of measures between different units.

Example

Each load of washing uses 100 g of powder. How many loads can be washed from a 2·5 kg box?

2·5 kg = 2500 g
2500 ÷ 100 = 25
Answer: *25 loads can be washed.*

A

1. A packet of cornflakes weighs one kilogram. 200 g is used. How much is left?

2. One lap of a running track is 400 m. How far is ten laps in kilometres?

3. There are three litres of water in a watering can. 540 ml is added. How much water is there in the can now?

4. Each parcel weighs 500 g. What is the weight of four parcels in kilograms?

5. Large pins are 3·5 cm long. Small pins are 15 mm shorter. How long are small pins?

6. Elsa buys a litre bottle of milk. She drinks half of the milk. How much is left in millilitres?

B

1. A door is 1·9 m tall. There is 76 cm from the top of the door to the ceiling. What is the height of the room?

2. A pile of 60 magazines weighs 10·8 kg. What does each magazine weigh in grams?

3. A tub of ice cream holds 2 litres. 350 ml is used. How much ice cream is left?

4. The fence round a square field is one kilometre long. What is the length of one side of the field in metres?

5. A pie weighs 1·5 kg. A larger pie weighs 735 g more. What is the weight of the larger pie?

6. Each tube of paint holds 40 ml. How much paint is needed to fill ninety tubes?

C

1. Twelve cartons of a drink hold a total of 2·7 litres. What does one carton hold in millilitres?

2. Myra buys 0·72 kg of mince. She uses 275 g. How much mince does she have left?

3. Each sheet of card is 1·5 mm thick. There are 50 sheets in a pack. How thick is a pack in centimetres?

4. A can of cycle oil holds 0·12 litres. 55 ml is used. How much oil is left?

5. Eight identical jars of sauce hold 2·8 kg of sauce. How much sauce is there in one jar in grams?

6. Gareth walks 765 m to the canal and 5·68 km along the towpath. How far does he walk altogether?

TARGET To solve 1-step and 2-step problems involving the conversion of measures between different units.

Example

A bottle contains half a litre of spray cleaner. 200 ml is used. Half of the rest is used. How much is left?
Answer: *150 ml is left.*

$\frac{1}{2}$ litre = 500 ml
500 ml − 200 ml = 300 ml
300 ml ÷ 2 = 150 ml

A

1. Jill throws the ball 28 m. Rae throws it 15 m further. What is the length of Rae's throw?

2. A bag of nuts weighs 100 g. 60g is eaten. How much is left?

3. Ian buys four pencils for £1. How much does each pencil cost?

4. A dishwasher uses 40 litres of water each wash. How much water does it use in five washes?

5. Josh has three 20p coins and three 10p coins. How much does he have altogether?

6. A piece of wood is 60 cm long. 10 cm is cut off. The rest of the wood is cut in half. How long are the two equal pieces?

B

1. One can of fish weighs 200 g. What do six cans weigh in kilograms?

2. Tiles are 20 cm long. How many are needed to make a row 4 m long?

3. Ricky buys two bottles of water, each holding 650 ml. He drinks half a litre. How much water does he have left?

4. A pie weighs 1 kg. It is cut into five equal slices. One is eaten. How much is left in grams?

5. Susan's daily paper costs 55p. Her Sunday paper costs £1·50. How much does she pay for her papers each week?

6. A drink is made with 1·2 litres of water and 300 ml of juice. It is then poured equally into 10 glasses. How much drink is in each glass?

C

1. A shower uses 6 litres of water in one minute. How much water does it use in one second?

2. A plank is 4 m long. Three 40 cm lengths are cut off. A further 75 cm is cut off. How long is the plank that is left?

3. A bath holds 38·7 litres of hot water and 11·6 litres of cold water. 800 ml evaporates. How much water is left in the bath?

4. One gravy cube weighs 6 g. What do 250 cubes weigh in kilograms?

5. An athlete runs 3·6 km to warm up, then a fast 800 m and 1·5 km to warm down. How far does she run altogether?

6. CDs cost £6·75. Lynne buys three for the price of two. How much has each CD cost her?

TARGET   To measure the perimeter of a 2-D shape.

The perimeter of a shape is the distance around its edges.

Examples

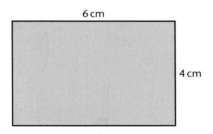

Perimeter of rectangle = (6 + 4 + 6 + 4) cm
= 20 cm

or

Perimeter of rectangle = 2(6 + 4) cm
= 2 × 10 cm
= 20 cm

Perimeter of hexagon
(2 + 1 + 2 + 3 + 4 + 4) cm = 16 cm

A

Measure the edges of each shape and work out the perimeters.

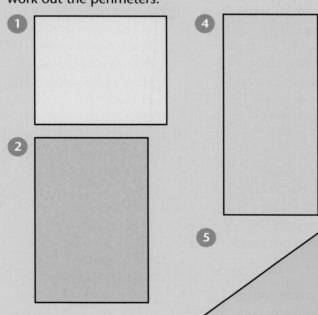

Use 1 cm squared paper.
Draw the following shapes and find the perimeter of each.

6 a rectangle
sides of 6 cm and 2 cm

7 a square
sides of 2 cm

8 a rectangle
sides of 4 cm and 3 cm

9 a square
sides of 5 cm

Use 1 cm squared paper.

10 Draw a square with a perimeter of 24 cm.

11 Draw a rectangle with a perimeter of 24 cm.

12 Draw 3 different rectangles each with a perimeter of 18 cm.

B

Measure the edges of each shape to the nearest millimetre. Work out their perimeters.

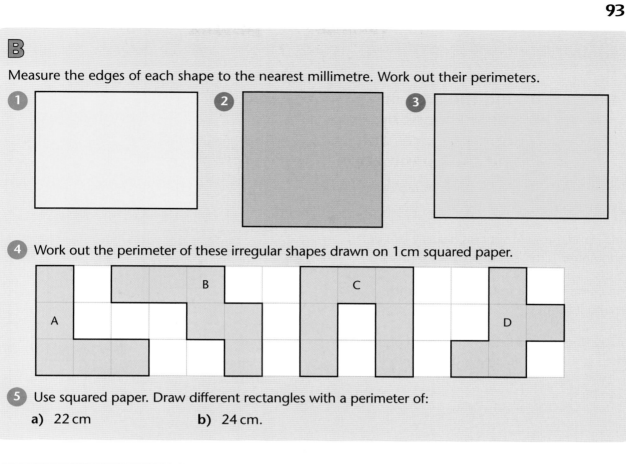

1

2

3

4 Work out the perimeter of these irregular shapes drawn on 1 cm squared paper.

A   B   C   D

5 Use squared paper. Draw different rectangles with a perimeter of:

a) 22 cm

b) 24 cm.

C

1 Copy and complete this table showing measurements of rectangles.

Length (cm)	9		7	10		11		12	35	
Width (cm)	3	2		4	8		8			4
Perimeter (cm)		16	20		34	26	50	42	100	36

Work out the perimeter of each shape. All the lengths are in centimetres.

2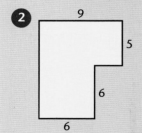
9
5
6
6

3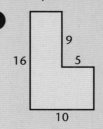
9
16
5
10

4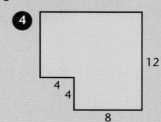
12
4
4
8

5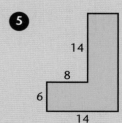
14
8
6
14

Use a set square and a ruler.
Draw the following rectangles and work out their perimeters.

6 3·3 cm by 5·7 cm

7 6·1 cm by 2·4 cm

8 4·8 cm by 7·2 cm

9 5·6 cm by 2·9 cm

TARGET To find the area of irregular shapes by counting squares and to find their perimeters.

The area of a shape is the amount of surface it covers.

Area is measured in squares, usually square centimetres (cm^2) or square metres (m^2).

The perimeter of a shape is the distance around its edges.

The perimeter of a field is the length of the fence around it. The area is the field itself.

Examples

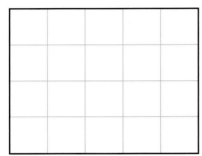

Area = 4 rows of five 1 cm^2
    = 20 cm^2
Perimeter = 2(5 + 4) cm
        = 2 × 9 cm
        = 18 cm

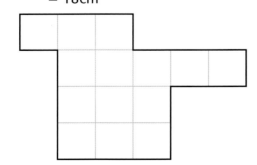

Area = 14 cm^2
Perimeter = 20 cm
(3 + 1 + 3 + 1 + 2 + 2 + 3 + 3 + 1 + 1) cm

A

Find the area of each of these irregular shapes.

①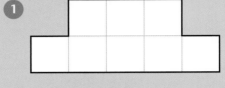

② 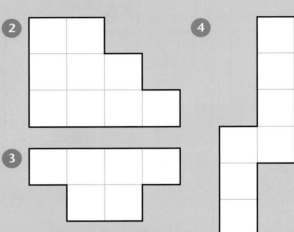 ④

③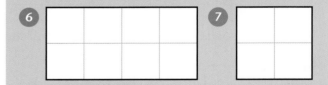

For each shape work out:

a) the area

b) the perimeter.

⑤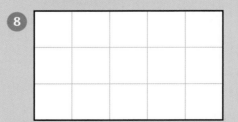

⑥   ⑦

⑧

⑨ Use squared paper.
Draw three different irregular shapes with an area of 8 cm^2.

B

For each of these irregular shapes work out:

a) the area

b) the perimeter.

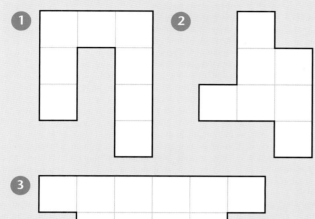

4 Draw three different rectangles with an area of 30 cm². Work out the perimeter of each.

5 Draw three different rectangles with a perimeter of 30 cm. Work out the area of each.

6 Use 1 cm squared paper. Draw three different irregular shapes with a perimeter of 18 cm. Work out the area of each.

7 Work out the area of each letter by counting squares and half squares.

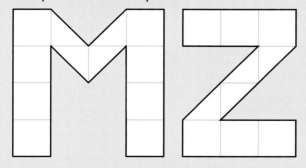

8 Make up your own drawings of letters using squared paper. Work out the areas.

C

Measure these shapes and work out their perimeters.

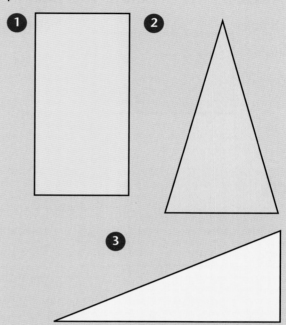

4 Copy and complete this table showing the measurements of rectangles.

Length	Width	Perimeter	Area
12 cm	3 cm		
8 cm		28 cm	
	5 cm		100 cm²
14 cm			28 cm²
	5 cm	24 cm	
		50 cm	24 cm²
	4 cm		64 cm²
		34 cm	70 cm²

5 How many square centimetres are there in a square metre?

6 Each square tile is 25 cm long. How many are needed to cover a wall 4 m long and 2 m tall?

7 A garden is 12 m wide and 30 m long. One quarter of the garden is a patio. What is the area of the rest of the garden?

TARGET   To calculate the perimeter of a 2-D shape.

Examples

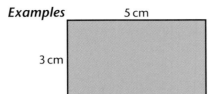

Perimeter = 2(5 + 3) cm
= 2 × 8 cm
= 16 cm

Perimeter = 36 cm

(10 + 8 + 6 + 4
+ 4 + 4) cm

A

Measure each shape and work out the perimeter.

1

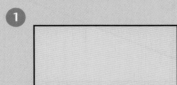

2

3

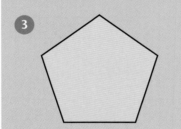

Work out the perimeter of each shape.

4 square
sides 9 cm

5 rectangle
sides 7 cm, 6 cm

6 equilateral triangle
sides 8 cm

7 regular pentagon
sides 5 cm

B

1 Copy and complete this table showing the measurements of rectangles.

Length	Width	Perimeter
8 cm	4 cm	
11 cm	6 cm	
6 cm	2 cm	
8 cm	7 cm	
10 cm	9 cm	
9 cm	5 cm	

For each of the following shapes work out:
a) the missing lengths *x* and *y*
b) the perimeter of the shape.

All lengths are in metres.

2

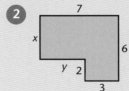

3
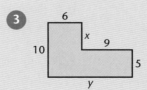

4
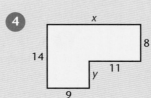

C

1 Copy and complete this table showing the measurements of rectangles.

Length	Width	Perimeter
16 cm		50 cm
4·5 cm	2 cm	
	5 cm	29 cm
11 cm		35 cm
5·7 cm	4·8 cm	
3·3 cm		10 cm

2 A room is 4 m wide and has a perimeter of 21 m.
a) How long is the room?
b) What is its area?

3 A field is 80 m long and has an area of 4000 m². How long is the fence around the field?

4 A square lawn has an area of 144 m².
It is enclosed by a path 1·5 m wide.
a) How long is the outer edge of the lawn?
b) How long is the outer edge of the path?

TARGET   **To find the area of a square or rectangle by multiplication.**

The area of a shape is the amount of surface it covers.
It is measured in squares, usually square centimetres (cm²) or square metres (m²).

Example

Area = 4 rows of six 1 cm²
    = 4 × 6 cm²
    = 24 cm²

Perimeter = (6 + 4 + 6 + 4) cm
        = 20 cm

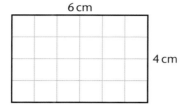

Area = length × width
    = (6 × 4) cm
    = 24 cm²

Perimeter = 2(6 + 4) cm
        = 2 × 10 cm
        = 20 cm

A

Use 1 cm squared paper.
Draw these shapes and
work out each area by
counting squares.

1. square
   sides 3 cm

2. rectangle
   sides 2 cm, 8 cm

3. square
   sides 5 cm

4. rectangle
   sides 7 cm, 3 cm

Use 1 cm squared paper.

5. Draw a square with an
   area of 16 cm².
   Work out the perimeter.

6. Draw a rectangle with
   a length of 7 cm and
   a perimeter of 26 cm.
   Work out the area.

7. Draw two different
   rectangles with an area
   of 12 cm².
   Work out the
   perimeters.

B

For each rectangle work out:
a) the area
b) the perimeter.

1.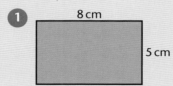

2.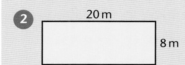

3. Copy and complete
   this table showing
   the measurements of
   rectangles.

Length	Width	Area
10 cm	8 cm	
7 cm	5 cm	
9 cm	6 cm	
11 cm	4 cm	
15 cm	2 cm	
12 cm	3 cm	

4. Use squared paper.
   Draw three different
   rectangles each with an
   area of 24 cm². Work
   out the perimeters.

C

For each of the following
rooms work out:
a) the area   b) the perimeter.

All lengths are in metres.

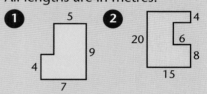

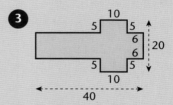

4. Copy and complete this
   table showing the length,
   width, perimeter and area
   of rectangles.
   All lengths are in cm.

L	W	P	A
8	6		
14			70
	3	40	
		28	45
12		30	
	6		90
		58	100
9		34	

TARGET To use mental methods to calculate measures and to convert between different units.

Examples

630 g + ☐ = 1 kg (1000 g)
Missing quantity is 370g

630 g → 700 g =   70 g
700 g → 1 kg   = 300 g
                 ─────
                 370 g

70 ml × 60 = ☐ litres
4200 ml = 4·2 litres

A

Work out mentally.

1. 85 cm + ☐ = 1 m
2. 35 cm + ☐ = 1 m
3. 500 g + ☐ = 1 kg
4. 700 g + ☐ = 1 kg
5. 900 ml + ☐ = 1 litre
6. 400 ml + ☐ = 1 litre

7. 32 m + 24 m
8. 9 m + 38 m
9. 56 kg + 36 kg
10. 14 kg + 75 kg
11. 48 litres + 23 litres
12. 21 litres + 67 litres

13. 70 m × 2 = ☐
14. 60 m × 5 = ☐
15. 80 ml × 4 = ☐
16. 50 ml × 3 = ☐
17. 30 g × 10 = ☐
18. 20 g × 8 = ☐

19. 240 m ÷ 3 = ☐ cm
20. 400 m ÷ 8 = ☐ cm
21. 80 g ÷ 2 = ☐ g
22. 700 g ÷ 10 = ☐ g
23. 450 ml ÷ 5 = ☐ ml
24. 120 ml ÷ 4 = ☐ ml

B

Work out mentally.

1. 27 cm + ☐ = 1 m
2. 84 cm + ☐ = 1 m
3. 650 ml + ☐ = 1 litre
4. 50 ml + ☐ = 1 litre
5. 350 g + ☐ = 1 kg
6. 550 g + ☐ = 1 kg

7. 1·3 m − ☐ = 95 cm
8. 1·2 m − ☐ = 53 cm
9. 1·7 kg − ☐ = 750 g
10. 1·4 kg − ☐ = 850 g
11. 1·1 litres − ☐ = 450 ml
12. 1·5 litres − ☐ = 650 ml

13. 20 cm × 60 = ☐ m
14. 300 m × 9 = ☐ km
15. 40 ml × 50 = ☐ litres
16. 700 ml × 8 = ☐ litres
17. 60 g × 30 = ☐ kg
18. 900 g × 7 = ☐ kg

19. 1·8 km ÷ 2 = ☐ m
20. 2·4 km ÷ 80 = ☐ m
21. 5·4 litres ÷ 9 = ☐ ml
22. 2·8 litres ÷ 40 = ☐ ml
23. 1·4 kg ÷ 7 = ☐ g
24. 4·8 kg ÷ 60 = ☐ g

C

Work out mentally.

1. 920 m + ☐ = 1 km
2. 480 m + ☐ = 1 km
3. 230 g + ☐ = 1 kg
4. 710 g + ☐ = 1 kg
5. 170 ml + ☐ = 1 litre
6. 660 ml + ☐ = 1 litre

7. 1·49 km − ☐ = 820 m
8. 1·15 km − ☐ = 590 m
9. 1·77 litres − ☐ = 930 ml
10. 1·34 litres − ☐ = 760 ml
11. 1·56 kg − ☐ = 610 g
12. 1·23 kg − ☐ = 470 g

13. 5000 m × 9 = ☐ km
14. 600 m × 70 = ☐ km
15. 900 g × 4 = ☐ kg
16. 40 g × 80 = ☐ kg
17. 8000 ml × 5 = ☐ litres
18. 900 ml × 60 = ☐ litres

19. 64 km ÷ 80 = ☐ m
20. 42 km ÷ 6 = ☐ m
21. 27 kg ÷ 300 = ☐ g
22. 35 kg ÷ 70 = ☐ g
23. 24 litres ÷ 4 = ☐ ml
24. 36 litres ÷ 900 = ☐ ml

TARGET   To add and subtract amounts of money using a written method.

Examples

```
      £
   3 9 · 7 5
 +   4 · 6 8
   4 4 · 4 3
     1   1   1
```

```
        £
    6  10  11  1
   7  1 · 2  0
 − 2 3 · 9 6
   4 7 · 2 4
```

A

Copy and complete.

1
```
      £
   4 · 4 5
 + 2 · 4 7
```

2
```
      £
   2 · 9 3
 + 1 · 4 5
```

3
```
      £
   7 · 6 8
 + 4 · 2 3
```

4
```
      £
   5 · 7 2
 + 3 · 6 5
```

5
```
      £
   9 · 5 4
 + 2 · 3 7
```

6
```
      £
   3 · 6 0
 + 1 · 8 6
```

7
```
      £
   3 · 7 3
 − 2 · 1 8
```

8
```
      £
   6 · 5 4
 − 3 · 9 2
```

9
```
      £
   2 · 6 0
 − 1 · 3 5
```

10
```
      £
   4 · 1 9
 − 2 · 7 3
```

11
```
      £
   5 · 8 4
 − 4 · 4 6
```

12
```
      £
   3 · 6 5
 − 1 · 8 1
```

13 Roy spends £6·82 in the butchers and £2·35 in the grocers. How much has he spent altogether?

14 Connie buys a present and a card for £9·74 altogether. The card costs £1·29. How much does the present cost?

B

Copy and complete.

1
```
       £
   1 6 · 7 4
 +   6 · 9 0
```

2
```
       £
   3 1 · 8 5
 + 2 7 · 8 5
```

3
```
       £
   5 3 · 4 9
 + 1 1 · 5 7
```

4
```
       £
   2 7 · 0 8
 + 2 3 · 5 6
```

5
```
       £
   4 5 · 6 2
 +   8 · 9 4
```

6
```
       £
   8 9 · 6 7
 + 3 9 · 2 7
```

7
```
       £
   1 8 · 2 9
 −   6 · 9 5
```

8
```
       £
   7 4 · 8 0
 − 1 5 · 7 3
```

9
```
       £
   5 6 · 5 8
 − 2 1 · 7 3
```

10
```
       £
   3 3 · 7 1
 − 1 6 · 3 5
```

11
```
       £
   4 7 · 2 6
 − 1 7 · 4 2
```

12
```
       £
   2 9 · 0 4
 − 2 0 · 6 9
```

13 A blue jacket costs £58·39. A green jacket costs £17·36 more than the blue. How much does the green jacket cost?

14 Richie has £61·75. He spends £28·92. How much does he have left?

C

Work out.

1 £292·54 + £13·69

2 £668·57 + £147·25

3 £349·68 + £123.52

4 £856·70 + £93·83

5 £793·86 + £280·57

6 £567·39 + £414·65

7 £161·48 − £53·80

8 £368·52 − £92·43

9 £270·95 − £124·27

10 £525·37 − £350·49

11 £315·74 − £248·07

12 £639·60 − £274·68

13 Bianca has £478·36 in her bank account and £65·85 in cash at home. How much does she have altogether?

14 The price of a necklace is £416·59. It is reduced by £127·90. What is the new price?

15 Each week Darcy earns £694·25 from his full time job and £176·68 from a part time job. How much does he earn altogether?

TARGET To multiply amounts of money using a written method.

Examples

$$
\begin{array}{r}
£ \\
5\cdot4\,7 \\
\times \qquad 9 \\
\hline
4\,9\cdot2\,3 \\
\scriptstyle 4 \quad 6
\end{array}
\qquad
\begin{array}{r}
£ \\
9\cdot2\,5 \\
\times \qquad 6 \\
\hline
5\,5\cdot5\,0 \\
\scriptstyle 1 \quad 3
\end{array}
$$

A

Copy and complete.

1
$$\begin{array}{r} £ \\ 0\cdot5\,3 \\ \times \qquad 2 \\ \hline \end{array}$$

7
$$\begin{array}{r} £ \\ 9\cdot6\,0 \\ \times \qquad 2 \\ \hline \end{array}$$

2
$$\begin{array}{r} £ \\ 0\cdot2\,7 \\ \times \qquad 8 \\ \hline \end{array}$$

8
$$\begin{array}{r} £ \\ 5\cdot3\,0 \\ \times \qquad 7 \\ \hline \end{array}$$

3
$$\begin{array}{r} £ \\ 0\cdot6\,4 \\ \times \qquad 5 \\ \hline \end{array}$$

9
$$\begin{array}{r} £ \\ 3\cdot7\,0 \\ \times \qquad 5 \\ \hline \end{array}$$

4
$$\begin{array}{r} £ \\ 0\cdot7\,5 \\ \times \qquad 3 \\ \hline \end{array}$$

10
$$\begin{array}{r} £ \\ 4\cdot8\,0 \\ \times \qquad 3 \\ \hline \end{array}$$

5
$$\begin{array}{r} £ \\ 0\cdot3\,9 \\ \times \qquad 6 \\ \hline \end{array}$$

11
$$\begin{array}{r} £ \\ 1\cdot6\,0 \\ \times \qquad 9 \\ \hline \end{array}$$

6
$$\begin{array}{r} £ \\ 0\cdot8\,2 \\ \times \qquad 4 \\ \hline \end{array}$$

12
$$\begin{array}{r} £ \\ 7\cdot4\,0 \\ \times \qquad 4 \\ \hline \end{array}$$

13 Each book costs £3·90. Ayesha buys three books. How much does she pay?

14 One stamp costs £0·49. What do eight stamps cost?

B

Copy and complete.

1
$$\begin{array}{r} £ \\ 1\cdot6\,8 \\ \times \qquad 6 \\ \hline \end{array}$$

7
$$\begin{array}{r} £ \\ 7\cdot5\,8 \\ \times \qquad 2 \\ \hline \end{array}$$

2
$$\begin{array}{r} £ \\ 3\cdot1\,9 \\ \times \qquad 4 \\ \hline \end{array}$$

8
$$\begin{array}{r} £ \\ 5\cdot7\,2 \\ \times \qquad 6 \\ \hline \end{array}$$

3
$$\begin{array}{r} £ \\ 2\cdot3\,7 \\ \times \qquad 9 \\ \hline \end{array}$$

9
$$\begin{array}{r} £ \\ 3\cdot1\,6 \\ \times \qquad 8 \\ \hline \end{array}$$

4
$$\begin{array}{r} £ \\ 4\cdot9\,5 \\ \times \qquad 8 \\ \hline \end{array}$$

10
$$\begin{array}{r} £ \\ 6\cdot9\,7 \\ \times \qquad 3 \\ \hline \end{array}$$

5
$$\begin{array}{r} £ \\ 5\cdot8\,1 \\ \times \qquad 5 \\ \hline \end{array}$$

11
$$\begin{array}{r} £ \\ 2\cdot6\,5 \\ \times \qquad 4 \\ \hline \end{array}$$

6
$$\begin{array}{r} £ \\ 6\cdot2\,9 \\ \times \qquad 7 \\ \hline \end{array}$$

12
$$\begin{array}{r} £ \\ 1\cdot8\,2 \\ \times \qquad 9 \\ \hline \end{array}$$

13 Lenny earns £8·45 each hour. How much does he earn if he works six hours?

14 Each tray of plants costs £5·27. What do four trays cost?

C

Work out.

1 £1847 × 7

2 £2196 × 5

3 £3904 × 9

4 £1782 × 8

5 £6419 × 6

6 £7538 × 3

7 £52·69 × 7

8 £16·75 × 9

9 £27·83 × 6

10 £85·92 × 4

11 £40·36 × 8

12 £34·78 × 7

13 A prize is shared between five friends. They each receive £58·64. How much is the prize?

14 A hotel room costs £69·25 per night. How much will it cost to stay for seven nights?

15 Hetty earns £3659 per month. How much does she earn in nine months?

16 What is the total cost of eight train tickets, each costing £28·95?

TARGET To divide amounts of money using a written method.

Examples

£4·55 ÷ 7

$$\begin{array}{r} £\,0\cdot65 \\ 7\overline{)\,£\,4\cdot{}^4\!5^3\!5} \end{array}$$ Answer £0·65

£70·00 ÷ 8

$$\begin{array}{r} £\quad8\cdot75 \\ 8\overline{)\,£\,7\,0\cdot{}^6\!0^4\!0} \end{array}$$ Answer £8·75

A

Copy and complete.

1. 4)£0·60
7. 2)£7·20

2. 2)£0·34
8. 9)£1·26

3. 6)£0·78
9. 5)£9·50

4. 5)£0·90
10. 7)£1·12

5. 8)£1·12
11. 3)£8·40

6. 4)£0·92
12. 8)£1·36

13. A toy costs £1·30. It is on sale for half price. How much will it cost?

14. A box of six eggs costs £1·50. What is the cost of each egg?

15. Kent buys three ice creams. He pays £2·37. How much does each ice cream cost?

B

Set out correctly.

1. £2·35 ÷ 5
2. £2·08 ÷ 8
3. £1·52 ÷ 4
4. £3·12 ÷ 6

5. £3·24 ÷ 9
6. £3·58 ÷ 2
7. £41·50 ÷ 5
8. £74·10 ÷ 3

9. £38·00 ÷ 4
10. £45·60 ÷ 8
11. £33·60 ÷ 7
12. £50·40 ÷ 6

13. A pack of eight yogurts costs £2·80. How much does each yogurt cost?

14. A £5 note is worth 7·35 US dollars. What is £1 worth in dollars?

15. Keri saves the same amount each week. In six weeks she saves £45. How much does she save weekly?

16. For four hours work Justin earns £25·60. How much is he paid each hour?

C

Set out correctly.

1. £14·68 ÷ 4
2. £47·52 ÷ 9
3. £39·44 ÷ 8
4. £34·25 ÷ 5

5. £27·78 ÷ 3
6. £21·49 ÷ 7
7. £383·40 ÷ 6
8. £194·00 ÷ 4

9. £463·50 ÷ 5
10. £341·10 ÷ 9
11. £465·60 ÷ 8
12. £207·20 ÷ 7

13. Nakia has saved one third of the £234·90 she needs to buy a bicycle. How much has she saved?

14. Albert orders a new carpet costing £487. He pays one fifth as a deposit. How much does he pay?

15. Nine members of Josie's family sponsor her 10p for each length of a pool swim. She raises £131·40 for charity. How many lengths did she swim?

TARGET To solve problems involving money using mental methods.

Example
A board games costs £6·50.
Nisha pays £10.
How much change is she given?

£6·50 → £7·00 = 50p
£7·00 → £10·00 = £3
Answer *£3·50 change is given.*

A

1. Sally has 37p. Vince has 58p. How much do they have altogether?

2. Apples are 30p each. How much do five cost?

3. Rahim has £4 in 50p coins. How many coins does he have?

4. Kirsty buys a magazine for 55p. She pays £1. How much change should she be given?

5. Seth has one 50p and three 5p coins. How much does he have altogether?

6. A bag of sweets costs 15p. A bar of chocolate costs three times as much. How much does the chocolate cost?

7. Alma buys four cards for £1·20. How much does one card cost?

8. A pear costs 35p. A banana costs 19p less. What is the price of a banana?

9. Chad has 25p more than Cliff. Cliff has 43p. How much does Chad have?

10. One can of peaches costs 40p. What do three cans cost?

B

1. Stamps cost 38p each. What do four stamps cost?

2. Denise buys some nuts. She pays £1 and receives 17p change. How much do the nuts cost?

3. Carlton travels to Manchester. His train fare is £39 return and his hotel costs £74. How much does his trip cost altogether?

4. A T-shirt costs £8·50. Nisha buys it for half price. How much does she pay?

5. Owen earns £47 a day for five days. How much does he earn altogether?

6. A cup of tea and a cake costs £1·60. The cake costs 85p. How much does the tea cost?

7. A small loaf of bread costs 79p. A large loaf costs 56p more. What is the price of a large loaf?

C

1. Damian buys three drinks for 60p each and a sandwich for £1·25. How much does he pay altogether?

2. A money bag holds £5 in 20p coins only. How many coins are there in the bag?

3. Elsa earns £11 per hour. In one week she works 37 hours. How much does she earn altogether?

4. Theo's shopping costs £14·35. He pays £20. How much change does he receive?

5. A flat costs £125 000. Another flat in the same block costs £7500 less. How much does the second flat cost?

6. Deanna's gym membership costs £600 for a year. How much does she pay each month?

7. Bus tickets cost £1·20. A travelcard costs £7·20 for 10 journeys. How much would you save by buying a travelcard?

8. One can of cat food costs 40p. How much do 80 cans cost?

TARGET   To solve problems involving money using mental methods.

Example

Chips cost £1·25. Fish costs £3·75. What is the cost of two pieces of fish and one portion of chips?

£3·75 × 2 = £7·50
£7·50 + £1·25 = £8·75
Answer *It costs £8·75.*

A

1. Five raffle tickets cost £1. What does one ticket cost?

2. Reggie buys a pen and a pencil for 80p altogether. The pencil costs 25p. How much does the pen cost?

3. Jacquie buys a rucksack for £49 and gloves for £26. How much does she pay altogether?

4. Chestnuts cost 9p each. How many can you buy with 50p? How much would you have left over?

5. Kirk has £102 in his wallet. He spends £8. How much does he have left?

6. Helen has seven 20p coins and one 50p coin. How much does she have altogether?

7. Cakes cost 50p each. A box of four cakes costs £1·60. How much would you save by buying a box?

B

1. Dean saves £40 each month for twelve months. How much does he save altogether?

2. Tiffany buys a postcard for 65p and a stamp for 48p. How much does she pay altogether?

3. Crayons cost 12p each. Myron's crayons cost £1·08 altogether. How many does he buy?

4. Joy has 35p in her pocket and five times as much in her purse. How much does she have altogether?

5. Max has 38p less than Fraser. Fraser has £1·24. How much does Max have?

6. Books cost £7. Maisie buys one and gets a second for half price. How much do her two books cost altogether?

7. Six ice creams cost £5·40 altogether. How much does one cost?

8. Jordan buys a chicken for £3·42. He pays £5. How much change does he receive?

C

1. Christy has £1000 in her bank account. She takes out £142. How much is left in the account?

2. Ellis buys six bars of soap for £2·10. How much does each bar cost?

3. Karla puts 50p into her piggy bank every week. How much does she save in 52 weeks?

4. Noel had £20 at the start of the day. He now has £11·68. How much has he spent?

5. Melissa and Naomi share a prize of £25·70. How much do they win each?

6. A TV set costs £615. In a sale its price is £498. How much has the price been cut?

7. A school buys eight new footballs for £11·40 each. How much do they cost altogether?

8. Theatre tickets cost £35. Children pay half price. What is the cost of tickets for two adults and three children?

TARGET To read, write and convert time between analogue and digital 12 and 24-hour clocks.

Analogue clocks have faces.
Read the minutes as:
past before 30 minutes
to after 30 minutes.

Digital clocks have figures only.
The minutes are always shown
as minutes past the hour.

12-hour clock time uses am and pm.
am means before 12 noon.
pm means after 12 noon.

24-hour clocks always have four
digits on display. Midnight is 00:00.

Examples

afternoon
4:38 pm

16:38

6:12
morning
6:12 am

06:12

A

Write each time shown to the nearest minute:

a) in words   **b)** in 12-hour clock time using am and pm.

1
night

5
morning

9
morning

13
night

17
evening

2 7:53
evening

6 2:06
afternoon

10 3:28
night

14 9:54
morning

18 6:12
morning

3
night

7
lunchtime

11
afternoon

15
breakfast

19
afternoon

4 4:39
afternoon

8 8:43
morning

12 11:24
night

16 1:05
lunchtime

20 10:51
morning

B

1 Copy and complete the table.

Time in words	12-hour clock	24-hour clock
4 minutes to 4 at night	3:56 am	03:56
		12:11
		17:43
		09:29
		13:57
	7:34 am	
	11:08 pm	
	2:41 am	
	8:59 pm	
18 minutes past 4 in the afternoon		
3 minutes past 6 in the morning		
24 minutes to 11 at night		
8 minutes to 1 at night		

2 For each of the above times work out how many minutes there are to the next hour.

C

Write each time shown to the nearest minute:

a) in words   b) in 12-hour clock time   c) in 24-hour clock time.

1 morning   **2** afternoon   **3**  night   **4**  night   **5** lunchtime

6 11:19 morning   **7** 5:55 afternoon   **8** 8:27 breakfast   **9** 1:38 night   **10** 9:45 night

11 For each of the above times work out how many hours and minutes there are to midnight.

12 Copy and complete the table showing flights from London Airport, changing the 12-hour clock times to 24-hour clock times. (All times are British.)

Destination	Athens	Beijing	Dubai	Miami	Mumbai	New York
Departure	1·20 pm	7·40 pm	9·10 am	2·20 pm	6·55 pm	8·45 am
Arrival	5·05 pm	5·35 am	4·00 pm	10·45 pm	4·20 am	3·10 pm
Flight Time	3 h 45 min					

TARGET To solve problems involving converting between units of time.

60 seconds = 1 minute
60 minutes = 1 hour
24 hours = 1 day
7 days = 1 week
12 months = 1 year

Example
How many hours make
240 minutes?
240 ÷ 60 = 4
Answer   *4 hours*

A

How many seconds make:

1. one minute

2. a quarter of a minute

3. one and a half minutes

4. three quarters of a minute?

How many minutes make:

5. one hour

6. one and a quarter hours

7. two and a half hours

8. four hours?

How many hours make:

9. one day

10. half a day

11. one and a quarter days

12. two days?

How many minutes are left in the hour if the time is:

13. quarter to the hour

14. half past the hour

15. quarter past the hour

16. 10 past the hour

17. 1 minute past the hour

18. 20 past the hour?

B

How many minutes are:

1. 120 seconds

2. 300 seconds

3. 330 seconds

4. 180 seconds?

How many hours are:

5. 90 minutes

6. 600 minutes

7. 120 minutes

8. 135 minutes?

How many minutes are left in the hour if the time is:

9. 4:25   13. 9:10

10. 11:40   14. 1:55

11. 8:05   15. 12:20

12. 2:35   16. 6:45?

How many hours are left in the day if the time is:

17. 2:00 pm

18. 5:00 am

19. 7:00 pm

20. 11:00 am?

21. How many hours are there in a week?

C

How many minutes are left in the hour if the time is:

1. 3:15   5. 8:21

2. 7:32   6. 4:46

3. 1:08   7. 11:19

4. 10:54   8. 5:33?

How many hours and minutes are left in the day if the time is:

9. 8:27 pm

10. 2:54 am

11. 3:39 pm

12. 9:02 am?

Write as days.

13. 4 weeks

14. 12 weeks

15. 240 hours

16. 60 hours

Write as years.

17. 7 decades

18. a quarter of a century

19. 48 months

20. 26 weeks

21. How many minutes are there in half a day?

22. How many hours are there in October?

TARGET To solve problems involving converting between units of time.

60 seconds = 1 minute
60 minutes = 1 hour
24 hours = 1 day
7 days = 1 week
12 months = 1 year

Example
What is the date two weeks
after March 23rd?
Answer   *April 6th*

March has 31 days.

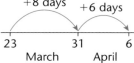

		+8 days		+6 days	
23			31		6
March				April	

A

☐ days has S_____,
A_____ J_____ and
N_____ .
All the rest have ☐,
Save for F _____ alone,
Which has but ☐ days clear,
And ☐ in each leap year.

1. Copy the above poem, writing the missing numbers and months.

2. How many days are there in:
   a) January
   b) February this year
   c) June
   d) October?

3. How many days are there:
   a) in a leap year
   b) in all other years?

4. When is the next leap year?

5. How many seconds make:
   a) 1 minute
   b) half a minute
   c) 2 minutes
   d) 10 minutes?

B

Copy and complete.

1. 90 minutes = ☐ hours
2. 300 minutes = ☐ hours
3. $1\frac{3}{4}$ hours = ☐ minutes
4. 8 hours = ☐ minutes
5. 14 days = ☐ weeks
6. 35 days = ☐ weeks
7. 20 weeks = ☐ days
8. 6 weeks = ☐ days
9. 36 months = ☐ years
10. 84 months = ☐ years
11. 50 years = ☐ months
12. $1\frac{1}{2}$ years = ☐ months
13. 240 hours = ☐ days
14. 36 hours = ☐ days
15. 2 days = ☐ hours
16. 7 days = ☐ hours

17. Give the date one week after:
    a) September 28th
    b) February 25th 2020.

18. Give the date two weeks before:
    a) February 10th
    b) July 6th.

C

1. How many seconds are there in:
   a) one hour
   b) 15 minutes?

2. How many minutes and seconds is:
   a) 150 seconds
   b) 1000 seconds?

3. How many hours and minutes are left in the day if the time is:
   a) 6:25 pm
   b) 11:41 am
   c) 2:07 pm
   d) 5:33 am?

4. It is Thursday 26th May. Give the date of:
   a) the second Sunday in June
   b) the last Wednesday in April.

5. If the 12th of December is a Monday, on which day of the week will fall:
   a) New Year's Eve
   b) St Andrew's Day (30th November)?

TARGET To solve word problems involving calculating lengths of time.

Examples

Jo leaves home at 8:40. She returns at 9:15. How long has she been out?

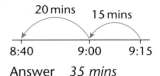

Answer *35 mins*

Ed is out 45 minutes. He returns at 2:20. When did he go out?

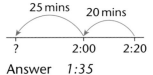

Answer *1:35*

A

1. David puts a cake in the oven at 1:10. He takes it out at 1:47. How long has it been in the oven?

2. A television programme begins at 4:15 and finishes at 5:00. How long does it last?

3. Hope answers the phone at 7:50. The call ends at 8:10. How long has she been talking to her friend?

4. Nigel begins drawing at 2:25. He finishes at 3:15. How long has he been drawing?

5. Assembly begins at 8:55. It ends at 9:25. How long does it last?

6. Dawn's piano lesson begins at 11:40. It ends at 12:35. How long does it last?

B

1. A plane is due to land at 6:30. It arrives 42 minutes late. When does it land?

2. Earl is on the bus for 34 minutes. He gets off at 2:15. When did he get on?

3. The Maths lesson starts at 9:55. It lasts 57 minutes. When does it finish?

4. Clara leaves school at 3:45. She arrives home at 4:18. How long does her journey take?

5. Tammy leaves the library at 5:05. She notices that she has been there 46 minutes. When did she arrive?

6. Hugo's CD lasts 69 minutes. He puts it on at 7:15. When will it finish?

7. A jacket potato will take 50 minutes to cook. It needs to be ready to eat at 12:30. When should it be put in the oven?

C

1. A film lasts 97 minutes. It finishes at 8:00. When does it start?

2. A tennis match starts at 11:09 and finishes at 12:25. How long has it lasted?

3. It starts to rain at 1:40. It rains for 110 minutes. When does it stop?

4. The train leaves Bristol at 8:16. It arrives in London at 9:45. How long has the journey taken?

5. The Brownies meeting lasts 115 minutes. It ends at 7:50. When does it start?

6. Wanda begins her paper round at 3:07. It takes her 85 minutes. When does she finish?

7. Jan finishes her horse ride at 11:32. She has been riding for 95 minutes. When did she set off?

TARGET   To solve word problems involving calculating lengths of time.

Examples

A lesson starts at 1:50.
It finishes at 2:25.
How long does it last?

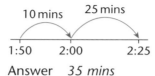

Answer   *35 mins*

A lesson starts at 10:30.
It lasts 50 minutes.
When does it finish?

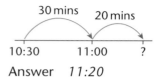

Answer   *11:20*

A

1. The television programme begins at 7:10. It finishes at 7:36. How long does it last?

2. The washing machine is switched on at 10:30. The wash ends at 10:52. How long does it take?

3. A train is due to arrive at 5:35. It is 18 minutes late. At what time does it arrive?

4. The PE lesson begins at 1:50. It finishes at 2:25. How long does it last?

5. It takes Jason half an hour to walk to school. He arrives at 8:45. When did he set off?

6. Gemma begins painting at 2:20. She finishes at 3:00. How long has she been painting?

B

1. Troy goes into the shopping centre at 11:44. He leaves 35 minutes later. When does he leave the centre?

2. Lara switches her computer on at 6:17. She switches it off at 7:10. How long is it on?

3. Paul needs to be at the airport at 9:30. The journey to the airport takes 45 minutes. At what time should he ask his taxi to arrive?

4. A netball game starts at 3:38. It lasts 40 minutes. When does it end?

5. Lunchtime lasts 55 minutes. It finishes at 1:05. When does it start?

6. Donna sets off for work at 7:55. Her journey takes 26 minutes. When does she arrive?

7. Robert takes his dog out for a walk at 09·23. They arrive back at 10·15. How long have they been out?

C

1. Glenn's bike ride lasts one and a half hours. He arrives home at 4:53. When did he set out?

2. The play rehearsal begins at 2:05. It lasts 76 minutes. When does it finish?

3. The class enter the museum at 10:25. They leave at 12:13. How long are they in the Museum?

4. Aisha wakes up at 5:40. She realises she has been asleep for 75 minutes. When did she fall asleep?

5. The film lasts 112 minutes. It starts at 7:15. At what time will it finish?

6. A chicken will take 100 minutes to cook. It needs to be ready to eat at 2:30. When should it be put in the oven?

7. The tennis match begins at 3·48. It lasts 2 hours 25 minutes. When does it finish?

TARGET   To compare and classify 2-D shapes.

A 2-D shape with straight sides is a polygon.

TRIANGLES

A 2-D shape with three straight sides is a triangle.

QUADRILATERALS

A 2-D shape with four straight sides is a quadrilateral.
Squares and rectangles are quadrilaterals.

OTHER POLYGONS

5 sides – pentagon
6 sides – hexagon
7 sides – heptagon
8 sides – octagon

A regular polygon has all sides and angles equal.

Example
Regular pentagon.

A

1 For each of the following shapes write down:
   a) the letter
   b) the number of sides
   c) the name of the shape.

A   B   C   D   E   F

      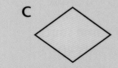

G   H   I   J   K   L

      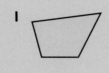

M   N   O   P   Q   R

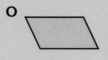   

2 Which of the above shapes have a right angle?

3 What is the largest possible number of right angles in:
   a) a triangle
   b) a quadrilateral
   c) a pentagon?

B

1

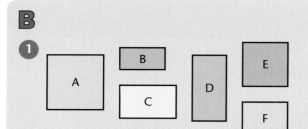

Which of the above shapes:

a) has the longest side
b) has the shortest side
c) has the largest area
d) has the smallest area?

2

Which of the above triangles:

a) has three equal sides
b) have two equal sides
c) have a right angle
d) have an obtuse angle?

Look at the shapes in Section A.
Write down the letter of all the shapes which:

3 are quadrilaterals

4 have 2 or more obtuse angles

5 have more than 2 lines of symmetry

6 have 1 or more pairs of parallel sides

7 have 2 or more acute angles

8 have 2 or more pairs of perpendicular sides

9 are not symmetrical

10 have 6 or more sides.

11 Draw a pentagon with:

a) 2 acute angles
b) 3 acute angles
c) 4 acute angles.

C

Copy the Carroll diagrams and use them to sort the shapes in Section A.

1

	more than 4 sides	not more than 4 sides
regular		
not regular		

2

	symmetrical	not symmetrical
less than 5 sides		
not less than 5 sides		

3 Copy or trace the symmetrical shapes in Section A. Draw on the lines of symmetry.

4 Use squared paper to draw the following shapes.

a) a quadrilateral with equal sides but not equal angles
b) a quadrilateral with one line of symmetry and two angles greater than 90°
c) a quadrilateral with one line of symmetry and one angle greater than 180°
d) a quadrilateral with one pair of parallel sides and no line of symmetry.

5 Draw a hexagon with two angles greater than 180°.

6 Draw a pentagon with two angles greater than 180°.

TARGET To compare and classify triangles.

TYPES OF TRIANGLE

equilateral
all sides equal
all angles equal

isosceles
2 sides equal
2 angles equal

right-angled
one 90° angle

scalene
no sides equal
no angles equal

A

Write the name of each triangle.

B

Which triangle is the odd one out?
Give a reason for your answer.

5 Use grids of 4 squares. Draw and label:
   a) 3 different right-angled triangles
   b) 2 different scalene triangles
   c) 4 different isosceles triangles.

Examples

 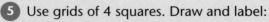

isosceles   right-angled
triangle   triangle

C

Example
Construct a triangle with sides 7 cm, 6 cm
and 5 cm using ruler and a pair of compasses.

1 Draw 7 cm line AB.

2 Draw arc 6 cm from A.

3 Draw arc 5 cm from B.

4 Join C, where
   arcs cross,
   to A and B.

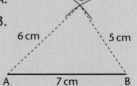

Use the above method to construct the
following triangles. Label each triangle.

1 Sides 4·6 cm, 4·6 cm, 4·6 cm

2 Sides 5·2 cm, 3·9 cm, 3·9 cm

3 Sides 6·4 cm, 5·7 cm, 2·8 cm

4 Sides 7 cm, 5·6 cm, 4·2 cm

5 Sides 5·5 cm, 5·5 cm, 3·3 cm

6 Sides 6·3 cm, 6·3 cm, 6·3 cm

7 Sides 6·5 cm, 6 cm, 2·5 cm

8 Sides 5·8 cm, 4·4 cm, 3·7 cm

TARGET   To compare and classify quadrilaterals.

TYPES OF QUADRILATERAL

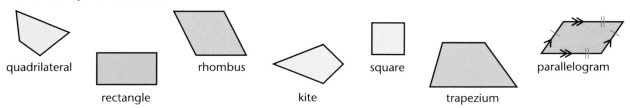

quadrilateral   rhombus   square   parallelogram

rectangle   kite   trapezium

A

1 Write down the name of each shape.

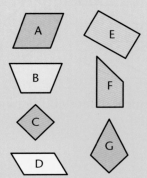

Copy and complete by writing the missing shape.

2 A .... has four equal sides and no right angle.

3 A .... has one pair of parallel sides.

4 A .... and a .... have two pairs of equal angles and two pairs of equal sides.

B

See the rhombus and parallelogram above for examples of:

• equal angles

• equal sides

• parallel sides →

1 Copy and label the six quadrilaterals with special names. For each shape:

   a) mark the equal angles.

   b) mark the equal sides.

   c) mark the parallel sides.

   d) draw on all the lines of symmetry.

2 Write down the name of all the quadrilaterals which have:

   a) 2 lines of symmetry only

   b) 0 lines of symmetry

   c) 2 pairs of equal angles

   d) 1 pair of equal angles

   e) 2 pairs of parallel sides

   f) 1 pair of parallel sides

   g) 4 equal sides

   h) 2 pairs of equal sides.

C

1 Use squared paper. Draw the following quadrilaterals using the intersections of the squares, but not using the lines.

   a) a rectangle

   b) a rhombus

   c) a symmetrical trapezium

   d) a square

   e) a parallelogram

   f) a trapezium which is not symmetrical

   g) a quadrilateral

   h) a kite

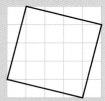

2 Draw on the diagonals of each shape. Which shapes have diagonals which:

   a) are of equal length

   b) bisect (cut each other in half)

   c) are perpendicular?

TARGET To identify lines of symmetry in 2-D shapes.

A shape is symmetrical if half of its shape matches the other half exactly. The line separating the two halves is the line of symmetry or mirror line.

Examples
One line of symmetry

Two lines of symmetry

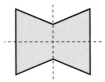

A

1 Which of these letters are not symmetrical?

R C T H P W
B Z M E F Y

2 Copy the symmetrical letters and draw on the line of symmetry.

3 Which of these shapes is not symmetrical?

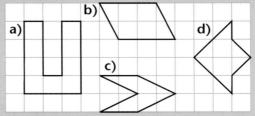

4 Copy the symmetrical shapes and draw on the line of symmetry.

B

1 Which of these shapes have:
   a) one line of symmetry
   b) no line of symmetry?

2 Which of these shapes has:
   a) two lines of symmetry
   b) four lines of symmetry?

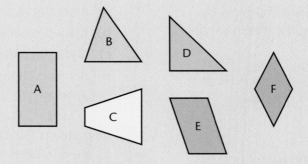

3 Use squared paper. Copy the symmetrical shapes. Draw on the line(s) of symmetry.

C

Use squared paper. Copy the shapes. Draw both lines of symmetry.

1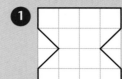

2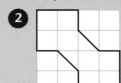

3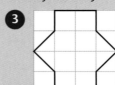

4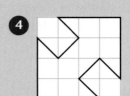

TARGET To draw 2-D shapes according to their properties and identify lines of symmetry.

A

Use triangular paper.

1 Copy these shapes and draw on any lines of symmetry.

2 Draw and label:
   a) an equilateral triangle
   b) a regular hexagon.
   Draw on any lines of symmetry.

Use squared paper.

3 Draw a quadrilateral:
   a) which has two pairs of equal sides but is not a rectangle
   b) which has four equal sides but is not a square.
   Draw on any lines of symmetry.

4 Draw different triangles and quadrilaterals on grids of 4 squares.

Examples

isosceles   quadrilateral
triangle

Label each shape and draw on any lines of symmetry as in the examples above.

B

Use triangular paper.

1 Draw and label a quadrilateral which is:
   a) symmetrical
   b) not symmetrical.

2 Draw and label a pentagon which is:
   a) symmetrical
   b) not symmetrical.

3 Draw and label a hexagon which is:
   a) symmetrical
   b) not symmetrical.

4 Draw on all the lines of symmetry in the shapes you have drawn.

5 Use squared paper. Draw different pentagons using the intersections of grids of 4 squares.

Examples

6 For each pentagon:
   a) draw on any lines of symmetry
   b) describe its features.

Example
Shape B has 2 pairs of equal sides, 3 right angles and 1 line of symmetry.

C

Use triangular paper.

1 Draw:
   a) a regular hexagon
   b) different hexagons which are symmetrical but not regular
   c) different hexagons which are not symmetrical.
   Draw on any lines of symmetry.

2 Investigate the different heptagons and octagons you can draw. Draw on any lines of symmetry. Label and describe the features of each shape.

3 Use squared paper. Using the intersections of grids of 4 squares, draw different hexagons. Draw on any lines of symmetry and describe the features of each shape.

4 Using the intersections of grids of 4 squares:
   a) how many different heptagons is it possible to draw
   b) how many different octagons is it possible to draw?
   Are any of the shapes symmetrical?

TARGET   To complete a symmetric figure with respect to a line of symmetry.

Examples

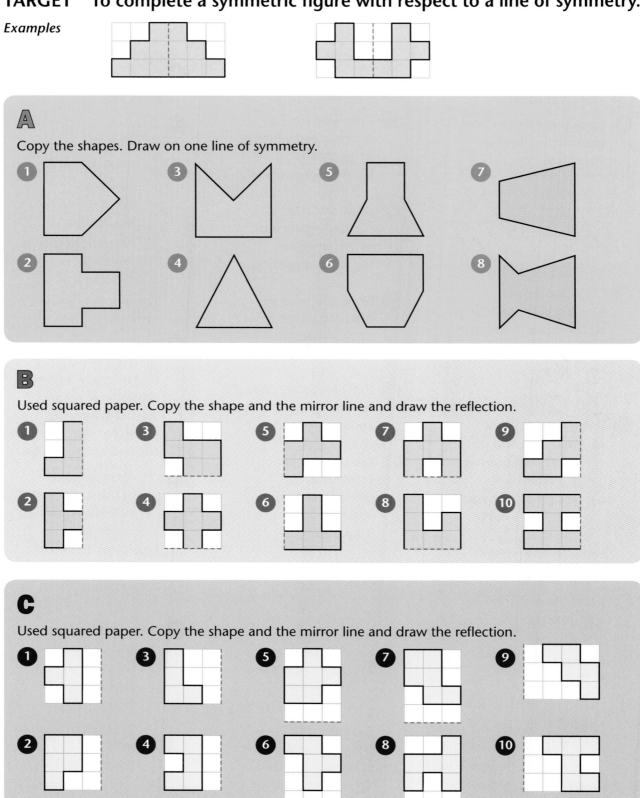

A

Copy the shapes. Draw on one line of symmetry.

B

Used squared paper. Copy the shape and the mirror line and draw the reflection.

C

Used squared paper. Copy the shape and the mirror line and draw the reflection.

TARGET   To complete symmetric patterns involving different orientations of lines of symmetry.

Examples

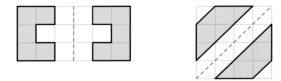

Used squared paper. Copy the shape and the mirror line. Sketch the reflection.

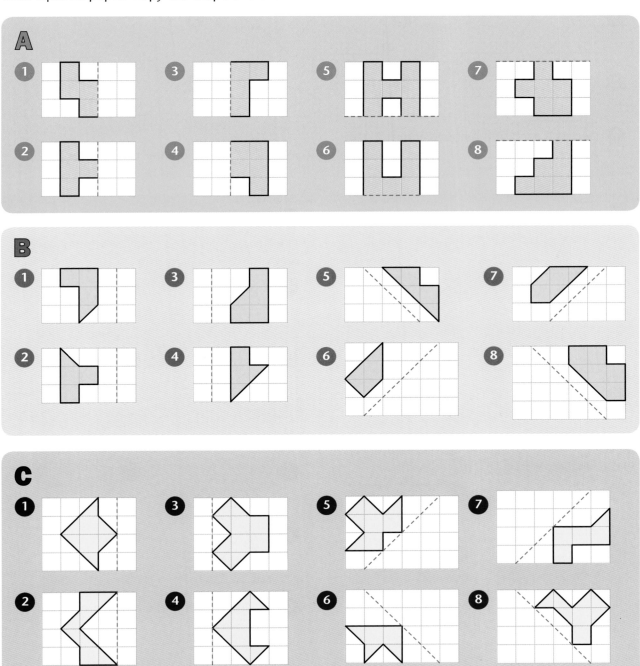

TARGET To compare and classify angles.

Examples

 right angle

 acute angle less than a right angle

obtuse angle greater than a right angle

A

Write down the larger of each pair of angles.

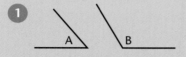 1

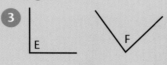 3

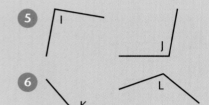 5

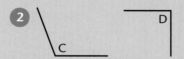 2

 4

6

7 Decide if each of the above angles A–L is:
   a) a right angle
   b) less than a right angle
   c) greater than a right angle.

B

Write each group of angles in order of size, smallest first.

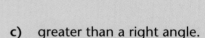 1

 2

 3

Place the angles in each shape in order of size, smallest first.

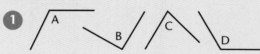 4   6

 5   7

8 Decide if each of the above angles A–Z is:
   a) a right angle   b) acute
   c) obtuse.

C

Place the angles meeting at each point in order of size, smallest first.

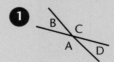 1   3

 2   4

Place the angles in each shape in order of size, smallest first.

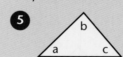 5   7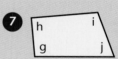

 6   8

9 Decide if each of the above angles A–P and a–n is:
   a) a right angle   b) acute
   c) obtuse.

TARGET   To describe positions on a 2-D grid.

A

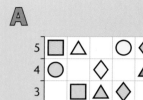

Give the position of each symbol.

1 △   **5** ◇

2 ◇   **6** ◇

3 △   **7** ▢

4 ⬤   **8** ▢

Draw the symbol found on each of these squares.

9 E5   **13** E1

10 C2   **14** A4

11 D1   **15** D5

12 B5   **16** E2

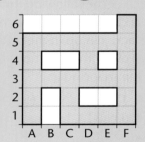

17 Give the position of:
  a) the door
  b) the chimney
  c) the downstairs window
  d) both upstairs windows.

B

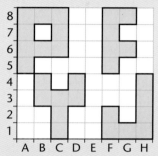

Give all the squares to describe the position of:

1 Y   **3** P

2 F   **4** J

Use an 8 × 8 grid like the one above. Shade in the following squares.

5 A7 B7 C7 A8 B8 C8

6 E2 F1 F2 G1 G2 H2

7 B2 B3 B4 C2 C3 C4 D4

8 F5 F6 G6 H6 H7

9 For each of your shapes write down:
  a) the name of the shape
  b) whether the shape is symmetrical or not.

10 Design three different letters in an 8 × 8 grid. Describe their position.

11 Design these numerals in an 8 × 8 grid and describe their position.

| 2 | 3 | 8 |

C

The position of a point on a grid is given by its co-ordinates. The across co-ordinate always comes first.

Examples

Q is (0, 2)   V is (4, 1)
N is (2, 0)   K is (1, 4)

Which letter is at point:

1 (3, 1)   **5** (4, 0)

2 (5, 5)   **6** (1, 2)

3 (0, 3)   **7** (3, 3)

4 (2, 4)   **8** (5, 0).

Give the position of:

9 A   **13** H

10 E   **14** K

11 P   **15** D

12 F   **16** B.

17 Write your name in co-ordinates.

18 Write the name of your school in co-ordinates.

TARGET To describe the position of a point on a grid by giving its co-ordinates.

The position of a point on a grid is given by its *x* and *y* co-ordinates.
The *x* co-ordinate always comes first.

Examples
Point R is (1, 3)
Point H is (3, 1)

A

Use the above grid.
Which letter is at point:

1 (1, 3)   **5** (2, 2)

2 (5, 1)   **6** (4, 3)

3 (0, 4)   **7** (5, 5)

4 (3, 5)   **8** (1, 0)?

Give the position of:

9 B   **13** X

10 Y   **14** F

11 O   **15** H

12 Q   **16** V.

Start at the co-ordinate given. Follow the direction. Write down the letter you find.

17 (5, 5)   Down 4

18 (3, 5)   Left 3

19 (3, 2)   Up 2

20 (0, 3)   Right 2

21 (4, 5)   Down 5

22 (5, 1)   Up 3

23 (4, 1)   Left 2

24 (1, 0)   Right 4

B

Use the above grid.
Write down the name spelled out.

1 (5, 1)   **4** (0, 4)
(4, 2)   (3, 1)
(0, 1)   (5, 4)
(2, 5)   (2, 3)

2 (5, 5)   **5** (1, 2)
(4, 3)   (4, 3)
(1, 0)   (5, 0)
(5, 0)   (2, 2)

3 (4, 0)   **6** (0, 1)
(2, 2)   (4, 2)
(0, 2)   (1, 3)
(5, 4)   (5, 4)
(2, 1)   (4, 4)

Start at the co-ordinate given. Follow the direction. Write down the letter you find.

7 (4, 5)   Left 2   Down 2

8 (0, 1)   Right 3   Up 4

9 (5, 3)   Left 4   Up 1

10 (2, 5)   Right 2   Down 3

11 (1, 0)   Right 4   Up 3

12 (4, 3)   Left 3   Down 2

C

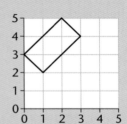

1 Copy the grid and the rectangle.

2 Draw the rectangle again moving each corner two squares right and two squares down.

3 Give the co-ordinates of:
   a) the first rectangle
   b) the second rectangle.

For each of the following, draw a 5 × 5 grid as above. Plot the points and join up in the order given. Follow the directions to draw the shape again.

4 (4, 1) (4, 2) (5, 3) (5, 0)
(4, 1)
Left 3 Up 1

5 (3, 4) (3, 5) (5, 5) (3, 4)
Left 2 Down 2

6 (1, 1) (2, 2) (4, 2) (3, 1)
(1, 1)
Right 1 Up 3

7 (0, 3) (1, 5) (2, 3) (0, 3)
Right 2 Down 3

TARGET   To plot points on a grid and draw sides to complete a given shape.

Example

Plot the following points and join them up in the order given. Identify and label the shape.
(1, 4) (2, 5) (4, 3) (3, 2) (1, 4)

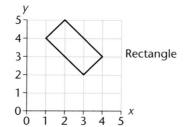

Rectangle

A

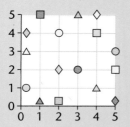

Draw the shape found at:

1. (4, 4)
5. (2, 2)
2. (0, 3)
6. (1, 0)
3. (5, 0)
7. (5, 3)
4. (3, 5)
8. (2, 4)

Give the position of each shape.

9. ⦾
13. ☐
10. ◇
14. ○
11. △
15. ☐
12. ◼
16. ◇

Follow the directions. Draw the shape you find.

17. Start at ⦾.
   Go Left 1 Up 2.

18. Start at △.
   Go Right 4 Down 2.

B

Draw a grid like the one above. Plot the points for each shape and join them up in the order given.

1. (0, 1)
   (1, 4)
   (2, 0)
   (0, 1)

2. (3, 2)
   (2, 4)
   (4, 5)
   (5, 3)
   (3, 2)

Draw a new grid and both shapes.

3. (1, 4)
   (3, 5)
   (2, 3)
   (0, 2)
   (1, 4)

4. (2, 1)
   (4, 3)
   (5, 2)
   (3, 0)
   (2, 1)

5. Identify and label each shape.

6.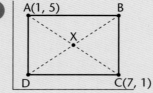

Write the co-ordinates of points B, D and X.

7. Write the co-ordinates of the mid-point of each side of the rectangle.

C

1. (1, 1), (2, 4) and (5, 3) are three corners of a square. What is the fourth corner?

2. Draw and label the axes of a 5 × 5 grid. Plot the above points and complete the square. Were you right?

3.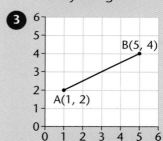

Copy the grid and the line. Complete a right-angled triangle ABC.

4. There are eight possible locations of C on the grid which will make a right-angled triangle. Can you find them all?

5. An isosceles triangle has two equal sides. Give the co-ordinates of the six possible locations of C on the grid which will make an isosceles triangle ABC.

TARGET   To describe movements between positions on a 2-D grid.

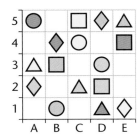

Examples
Start at A5, (⬤)
Go Right 2 squares.
Draw the symbol.

Answer ☐

Start at D1. (▲)
Go Left 3 squares.
Now go Up 2 squares.
Draw the symbol.

Answer △

A

Use the above grid.
Draw the symbol found on
each of these squares.

1 C4   **5** E4

2 A5   **6** C5

3 D1   **7** A3

4 B3   **8** D2

Follow the directions.
Draw the symbol you find.

9 Start at E4.
Go Down 3 squares.

10 Start at B3.
Go Right 2 squares.

11 Start at C2.
Go Up 3 squares.

12 Start at E2.
Go Left 4 squares.

13 Start at D4.
Go Down 3 squares.

14 Start at A4.
Go Right 4 squares.

15 Start at C3.
Go Left 2 squares.

B

Use the above grid.
Give the positions of these
symbols.

1 ◇   **5** ◆

2 ◇   **6** △

3 ◇   **7** ○

4 △   **8** ○

Follow the directions.
Draw the symbol you find
at the end.

9 Start at B3.
Right 3 squares.
Up 2 squares.

10 Start at D4.
Down 2 squares.
Left 3 squares.

11 Start at E1.
Up 2 squares.
Left 4 squares.

12 Start at A5.
Down 3 squares.
Right 2 squares.

13 Start at C2.
Left 2 squares.
Up 3 squares.

C

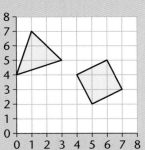

Copy and complete the
co-ordinates of each shape.

1 Triangle   **2** Square
(0, 4)   (4, 4)
(1, ☐)   (6, 5)
(☐, ☐)   (7, ☐)
                  (☐, ☐)

3 Copy the grid and
the triangle. Draw the
shape again moving
each point:
Right 2 Down 4

4 Copy the grid and
the square. Draw the
shape again moving
each point:
Left 3 Up 2

5 Give the co-ordinates
of its new position for
each shape.

TARGET To describe movements between positions on a grid as co-ordinates.

To translate a shape means to slide it into a new position. Every point of the shape moves:

a) the same distance

b) in the same direction.

Example

Translate the orange triangle:

① Down 3 (D3)

② Right 2 Down 1 (R2 D1).

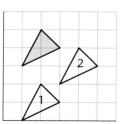

A

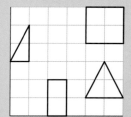

① Copy the grid and the square.
Translate the square:

a) Left 3 (L3)

b) Down 4 (D4)

② Copy the grid and the rectangle.
Translate the rectangle:

a) Up 3 (U3)

b) Right 2 (R2)

③ Copy the grid and the right-angled triangle.
Translate the triangle:

a) Down 2 (D2)

b) Right 4 (R4)

④ Copy the grid and the isosceles triangle.
Translate the triangle:

a) Up 2 (U2)

b) Left 4 (L4)

B

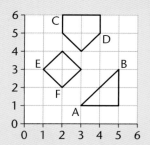

① Copy the grid and the triangle. Translate the shape:

a) L2 U2   **b)** R1 U3

② Copy the grid and the pentagon. Translate the shape:

a) L1 D2   **b)** R2 D4

③ Copy the grid and the square. Translate the shape:

a) L1 U2   **b)** R3 D1

④ Give the co-ordinates of the position of each letter A–F:

a) in the above shape

b) in the translations.

C

① Copy the grid in Section B.
Plot these co-ordinates and join them up in the order given to draw a triangle.
(1, 4) (2, 6) (3, 3) (1, 4)
Translate the shape:

a) R2 D1   **b)** L1 D3

② Give the co-ordinates of the new position of the triangle for each translation.

③ Draw another grid and plot these co-ordinates.
(3, 2) (4, 4) (5, 4) (4, 2) (3, 2)
Join them up in the order given to draw a parallelogram.
Translate the shape:

a) R1 U2   **b)** L3 D1

④ Give the co-ordinates of the new position of the parallelogram for each translation.

TARGET To present data in a bar chart.

Example

A shop sells the following flavours of ice cream.

Banana

Chocolate

Mint

Peach

Strawberry

Vanilla

This table shows the number of portions of each flavour sold in one day.

Flavour	Portions sold
Banana	25
Chocolate	45
Mint	35
Peach	15
Strawberry	20
Vanilla	40

The data in the table can be presented in a bar chart.

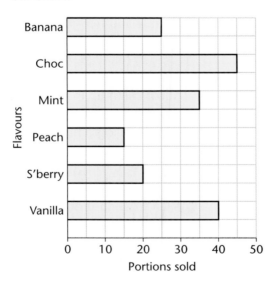

A

1 The children in one class voted for their favourite topic from those they had studied in the year. These are the results.

Topic	Number of votes
Space	5
Dinosaurs	9
Romans	7
Jungles	3
Rivers	6

Draw a bar chart to show the results.

2 This table shows the time taken by six children to find their way out of a maze.

Names	Time (minutes)
Kieran	18
Ivan	8
Franny	24
Delisha	12
Arnav	20
Lauren	14

Draw a bar chart to show the results. Label the bar graph in twos.

B

1 The members of a swimming club were asked to choose one activity each in which they would like individual coaching. These are the results.

Activity	Number of choices
Diving	40
Backstroke	15
Breaststroke	30
Front crawl	35
Life saving	55

Draw an horizontal bar chart labelled in fives to show the results.

2 This table shows the flowers used to make a floral display.

Colour	Number of flowers
Blue	70
Mauve	55
Orange	40
Red	30
White	100
Yellow	75

Draw a vertical bar chart labelled in tens to show the information.

C

1 This table shows the names used for roads in a town.

Name of road	Frequency
Avenue	130
Crescent	50
Drive	80
Road	160
Street	190
Terrace	30
Others	70

Draw an horizontal bar chart labelled in 20s to show the information.

2 This table shows the number of bottles of milk sold each day in a supermarket.

Day of week	Number of bottles
Monday	850
Tuesday	700
Wednesday	550
Thursday	450
Friday	900
Saturday	1050
Sunday	400

Draw a vertical bar chart labelled in 100s to show the data.

TARGET To solve problems using information presented in pictograms.

Example

This pictogram shows the number of T-shirts of different sizes sold in a large department store in one month.

Size

XS 👕 👕 ▌

S 👕 👕 👕 👕

M 👕 👕 👕 👕 👕 👕 ▌

L 👕 👕 👕 👕 👕

XL 👕 👕 👕

XXL 👕 ▌

👕 represents 100 T-shirts

1. Which size sold the fewest shirts?
XXL

2. How many medium size shirts were sold?
650

3. How many more large shirts were sold than extra large?
200 (500 − 300)

4. How many fewer extra small shirts were sold than small?
150 (400 − 250)

5. How many shirts smaller than a medium were sold?
650 (250 + 400)

6. How many shirts larger than a medium were sold?
950 (500 + 300 + 150)

A

This pictogram shows the number of chess matches won by 6 children from one school taking part in a week long chess tournament.

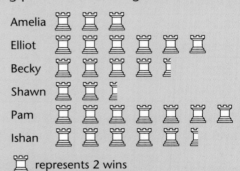

♜ represents 2 wins

1. Who won the most games?

2. Who won the least games?

3. How many games did Ishan win?

4. Who won nine games?

5. How many more games did Elliot win than Becky?

6. How many fewer games did Shawn win than Pam?

7. How many games were won by the three girls altogether?

8. How many games were won by the three boys altogether?

B

This pictogram shows the number of students learning to play different instruments at a music college. Each student chose one instrument only.

Cello	♫ ♫ ♫ ♫
Flute	♫ ♫ ♪
Guitar	♫ ♫ ♫ ♫ ♫ ♫ ♫ ♪
Piano	♫ ♫ ♫ ♫ ♫ ♫ ♫
Trumpet	♫ ♫ ♪
Violin	♫ ♫ ♫ ♫ ♫ ♪

♫ represents 10 students

1. Which instrument was being studied by more students than any other?

2. Which instrument was being studied by fewest students?

3. How many students were learning:
   a) the violin   b) the cello?

4. Which instrument was being studied by:
   a) 75 students   b) 30 students?

5. How many more students were learning the cello than the flute?

6. How many more students were learning the piano than the violin?

7. How many students were studying either of the wind instruments?

8. How many students were studying an instrument played with a bow?

9. Altogether how many students were studying an instrument?

10. Which instrument would you learn to play?

C

This pictogram shows the number of crates of apples of different types sold in a supermarket in six weeks.

Braeburn	🍎 🍎 🍎 🍎 🍎 🍎 ◖
Cox's	🍎 🍎 🍎 ◖
Delicious	🍎 🍎 🍎 🍎 🍎 ◖
Gala	🍎 🍎 🍎 🍎 🍎 🍎 🍎
Jazz	🍎 🍎 🍎 🍎
Pink Lady	🍎 ◖

🍎 represents 50 crates

1. Of which type of apple were 200 crates sold?

2. How many Cox's apples were sold?

3. Of which type of apple were 325 crates sold?

4. How many pink lady apples were sold?

5. How many more Gala apples were sold than Delicious?

6. How many fewer Cox's than Braeburn were sold?

7. How many crates were sold of the two best selling varieties combined?

8. Jazz and Pink Lady had combined sales which were the same as which other variety?

9. How many crates of apples were sold altogether?

TARGET   To interpret data presented in a bar chart.

Visitors to a zoo were asked to choose which of the animals they had found most interesting. These are the results.

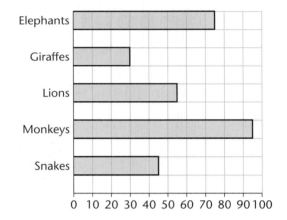

Look at the bar chart.

1 What is the value of:
   a) one division   *10 visitors*
   b) half a division?   *5 visitors*

2 How many visitors chose the elephants?   *75*

3 Which animals were chosen by 45 visitors?   *snakes*

4 How many more visitors chose the elephants than the giraffes?   *45*

5 How many fewer visitors chose the lions than the monkeys?   *40*

6 How many visitors voted?
   (45 + 95 + 55 + 30 + 75)   *300*

A

This bar chart shows the type of weather recorded for each day of one complete month.

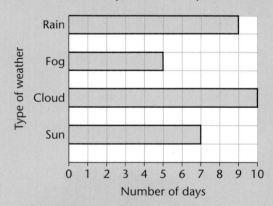

1 Which type of weather was recorded least often?

2 Which type of weather was recorded most often?

3 How many days of the month were sunny?

4 Which type of weather was recorded on 9 days?

5 How many more days were cloudy than sunny?

6 On how many fewer days was there fog than rain?

7 How many days were there in the month?

8 The name of the month has eight letters. Which month is it?

B

This bar chart shows the number of drinks sold in a café in one day.

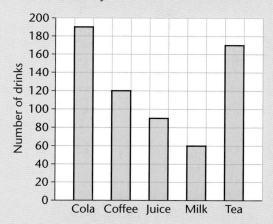

1. Which drink was sold:
   a) most often
   b) least often?

2. Which drink was bought by 60 people?

3. How many fruit juices were sold?

4. Which drink was bought by 170 people?

5. How many colas were sold?

6. How many more teas were bought than coffees?

7. How many fewer milks were bought than colas?

8. How many hot drinks were sold altogether?

9. How many cold drinks were sold altogether?

C

This bar chart shows the number of customers using a large shopping mall in one week.

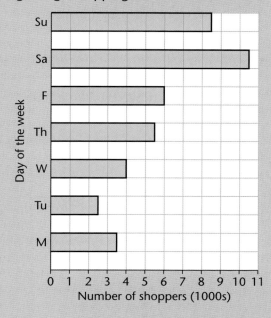

1. On which day did 5500 shoppers use the mall?

2. Which day had the most shoppers?

3. How many people used the mall on Wednesday?

4. How many more shoppers were there on Monday than Tuesday?

5. How many fewer shoppers were there on Friday than Sunday?

6. How many more people used the mall on the busiest day of the week than on the least busy?

7. How many people used the mall:
   a) at the weekend
   b) on the five school days altogether?

TARGET　To solve problems using information presented in bar charts.

Example

This bar chart shows the size of the audience at each of the five performances of an ice show (Tuesday to Saturday).

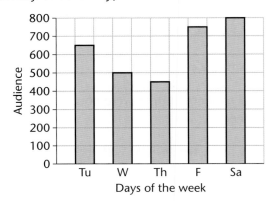

1　How many people saw the show on Thursday?　　　　　*450*

2　How many more people saw the show on Tuesday than on Wednesday?

150 (650 − 500)

3　How many fewer people saw the show on Friday than Saturday?　*50 (800 − 750)*

4　What was the total audience:

a)　for the last 2 performances

1550 (800 + 750)

b)　for the first 3 performances?

1600 (650 + 500 + 450)

A

The members of a football club were each asked to choose the skill which they thought was their greatest strength. These are the results.

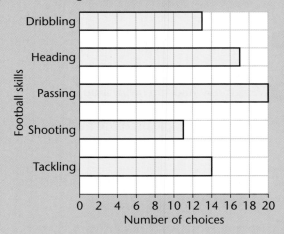

1　Which skill was chosen most often?

2　Which skill was chosen least often?

3　How many club members chose tackling?

4　Which skill was chosen by 11 members?

5　How many members chose dribbling?

6　Which skill was chosen by 20 members?

7　How many fewer members chose dribbling than heading?

8　How many more members chose passing than shooting?

9　How many of the club's players took part in the survey?

10　Which skill would you choose?

B

This bar chart shows the length of Class 5's lessons on one Tuesday.

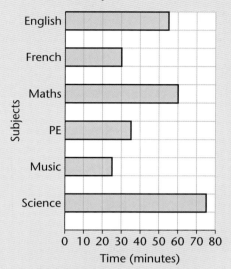

1 Which was the shortest lesson?

2 Which was the longest lesson?

3 How long was the English lesson?

4 Which lesson lasted 35 minutes?

5 How long was Music?

6 Which lesson lasted half an hour?

7 How much longer was PE than Music?

8 How much shorter was Maths than Science?

9 English, French and Maths were taught in the morning; the other three classes in the afternoon. How long were:
   a) the morning lessons
   b) the afternoon lessons?

10 How much longer altogether were the Maths and Science lessons than the English and French?

C

This bar chart shows the number of votes cast for each dance in a televised celebrity dancing competition.

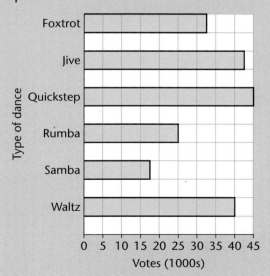

1 Which dance received 17 500 votes?

2 How many people voted for the jive?

3 How many more people voted for the waltz than the rumba?

4 How many fewer people voted for the foxtrot than the quickstep?

5 What was the difference between the number of votes received by the most popular dance and the least popular?

6 How many people altogether voted for one of the three Latin dances: the jive, the rumba and the samba?

7 How many more people voted for one of the three Ballroom dances than for one of the Latin dances?

8 How many people voted altogether?

TARGET   To interpret and present continuous data.

DISCRETE DATA

Discrete means separate. Discrete data is organised in separate categories. e.g. colours, countries, favourite drinks, etc. Discrete data is often presented in a bar chart.

The colours of 100 jackets sold in a menswear shop.

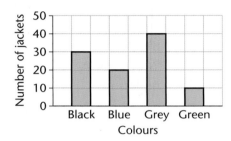

Each colour is a discrete category. This is shown by having gaps between the bars.

CONTINUOUS DATA

With continuous data each category is not separate but runs into the next one. Continuous data often consists of measurements organised into ranges of values, e.g. heights, weights, distances, times, etc. It can be presented in a type of bar graph called a histogram.

The distances thrown by 100 children in a cricket ball throwing competition.

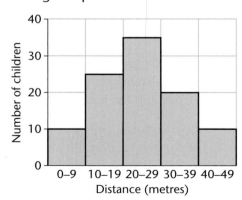

The ranges are continuous. This is shown by having no gaps between the bars.

This bar chart shows how the children in a village school travel to school each morning.

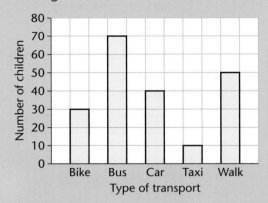

1. What is the value of one division?

2. How many children come to school by bike?

3. How many more children come to school by bus than by car?

4. Which form of transport is used by the least children?

5. How did 50 of the children come to school?

6. How many children are there in the school altogether?

7. This table shows the number of people using a swimming pool in one day.

Pool users	Number of users
Boys	75
Girls	60
Men	55
Women	100

Draw a bar chart labelled in tens to show the information in the table.

B

This bar graph shows the ages of the guests at a wedding.

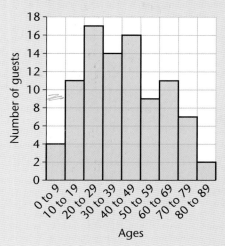

C

This bar graph shows the heights of the children in Year 4.

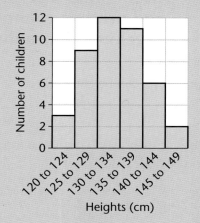

1 How many of the guests were:

a) in their seventies

b) under 10?

2 How many more of the guests were in their 20s than their 30s?

3 How many fewer of the guests were in their 50s than their 60s?

4 How many of the guests were:

a) 60 or over

b) under 20?

5 How many guests were at the wedding altogether?

6 This table shows the turnover (total sales) of a cafe in its first six months of trading.

Month	Turnover (£)
March	3000
April	2500
May	4000
June	5500
July	7500
August	9000

Draw an histogram labelled in 1000s to present the data in the table.

1 How many of the children are:

a) less than 130 cm tall

b) more than 139 cm tall?

2 How many more children are between 130 and 134 cm tall than are between 135 and 139 cm tall?

3 How many more of the children are in the 140–144 cm range than are in the 145–149 cm range?

4 How many children are there in Year 4 altogether?

5 This table shows the weights of two hundred 18 year old men applying to join the army.

Weight (kg)	Men
50–59	35
60–69	55
70–79	70
80–89	25
90–99	10
100–109	5

Draw an histogram labelled in 10s to show the data in the table.

TARGET To begin to interpret and present change over time in graphs.

HISTOGRAMS

Change over time can be shown in an histogram.

Example

The number of spectators entering a football ground in the hour before kick off.

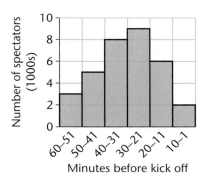

Look at the histogram.

1. How many spectators entered the ground in the first 20 minutes of the hour before kick off?

   Answer *8000* (3000 + 5000)

2. How many fewer spectators entered the ground in the final 10 minutes before kick off than in the 10 minute period before it?

   Answer *4000* (6000 − 2000)

3. How many more spectators entered the ground in the last half hour before kick off than in the half hour before it?

   Answer *1000* (17 000 − 16 000)

Tanith and Ricky always tried to guess which colour pen their teacher would use for a whiteboard. One half term they recorded the colours used. These are the results.

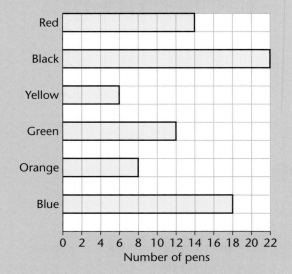

1. Which colour pen was used least often?

2. How many times was the orange pen used?

3. Which colour pen was used 12 times?

4. How many more times was the blue pen used than the orange?

5. How many fewer times was the red pen used than the black?

6. Tanith said that their teacher used either a blue or a black pen half the time. Was she right? Explain your answer.

7. This table shows the number of chickens sold in a butcher's shop in five days.

Days	Tues	Wed	Thur	Fri	Sat
Chickens	3	6	2	9	7

   Draw a bar chart labelled in twos to show the information.

B

This graph shows the average daily maximum temperature recorded in Birmingham for one year.

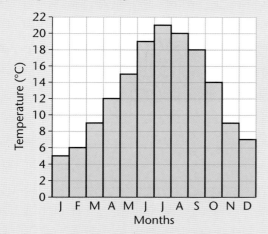

1 What was the temperature in:

a) October   b) March?

2 In which two months was the temperature 9°C?

3 Between which two months was there:

a) the largest rise in temperature

b) the largest fall in temperature?

4 How much higher was the average temperature:

a) in May than in April

b) in July than in January?

5 This table shows the temperature recorded every two hours for one day in March?

Time	Temp (°C)	Time	Temp (°C)
00:00	4	14:00	15
02:00	1	16:00	14
04:00	−1	18:00	11
06:00	−2	20:00	8
08:00	0	22:00	5
10:00	6	00:00	3
12:00	11		

Draw an histogram labelled in twos to show the information in the table.

C

This line graph shows the journey of a family from their home by bus, train and coach to their holiday destination in the New Forest.

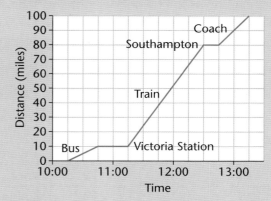

1 At what time did the family board the bus?

2 What was the length of the bus journey to Victoria Station?

3 How long did they wait at the station before the train departed?

4 How far is it from Victoria Station to Southampton?

5 When did the train reach Southampton?

6 How long did the coach journey take?

7 From home to holiday destination:

a) what was the total distance travelled

b) how long did the whole journey take?

8 Draw a line graph to show each of the two sets of data in Section B.

Example
Average daily maximum temperature (Birmingham)

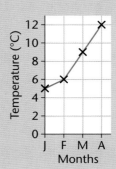

TARGET   To solve problems using information presented in tables.

This table shows the height, weight and shoe size of 12 children recorded when they were in Year 2 and again when they were in Year 3.

	YEAR 2				YEAR 3	
Height (cm)	Weight (kg)	Shoe size	Name	Height (cm)	Weight (kg)	Shoe size
119	24	13	Erin	125	28	2
129	28	2	William	137	31	3
122	23	1	Ameera	127	26	1
116	20	12	Lance	120	22	1
125	25	13	Minnie	131	29	2
130	29	1	Camille	136	31	3
121	21	13	Jordan	125	23	2
129	27	1	Alfie	135	32	2
113	19	13	Lynda	118	23	1
126	26	13	Ryan	131	29	2
123	24	1	Tyrone	130	28	3
118	23	13	Courtney	123	25	1

A

Look at the data for Year 2 only.
Write down:

1 Lynda's shoe size

2 Ameera's height

3 Camille's weight

4 Tyrone's shoe size

5 William's height

6 Alfie's weight

7 Courtney's shoe size

8 Minnie's height

Look at the data for Year 3 only.
Write down:

9 Ryan's weight

10 Lance's height

11 Erin's shoe size

12 Jordan's weight

13 Courtney's height

14 Ameera's shoe size

15 William's weight

16 Alfie's height

B

Look at the data for Year 2 only.

1 Who was:
   a) the tallest   b) the shortest?

2 Who had the smallest shoe size?

3 How many children weighed:
   a) more than 25 kg
   b) less than 25 kg?

4 Who was the same height as Alfie?

5 Which children wore Size 1 shoes?

6 Who was 5 cm shorter than Ryan?

7 What was the difference between the weight of Ameera and Courtney?

8 What was the largest shoe size?

9 How many children were:
   a) taller than 125 cm
   b) shorter than 125 cm?

Look at the Year 3 data only.

10 Who was the tallest?

11 Who was:
   a) the lightest   b) the heaviest?

12 How many children were:
   a) taller than 125 cm
   b) shorter than 125 cm?

13 Which children wore Size 1 shoes?

14 Who weighed the same as Tyrone?

15 Which children were taller than Minnie?

16 Who weighed 5 kg less than Camille?

17 Which children had the same shoe size as William?

18 How many children weighed:
   a) more than 25 kg
   b) less than 25 kg?

C

Look at the data for both Year 2 and Year 3.

1 Who had not changed shoe size?

2 How much had Jordan gained:
   a) in height
   b) in weight?

3 How many children had increased from Size 13 shoes to Size 1?

4 Who had gained more height?
   a) Erin or Ryan
   b) Tyrone or Alfie

5 Who had gained most weight?
   a) Courtney or Lynda
   b) Minnie or Camille?

6 How many children had gone up two shoe sizes?

7 Which children had increased in height by more than 5 cm?

8 Which children had increased in weight by less than 3 kg?

9 Who had gained the most:
   a) in height
   b) in weight?

10 Which two children had gained least in height?

11 Which children wore the most common shoe size in both Year 2 and Year 3?

12 Which children had gained the same amount of weight as William?

Write in figures.

1. two thousand six hundred and thirty-four

2. five thousand and seventy-two

3. nine thousand two hundred and fifty

4. four thousand seven hundred and six

Write in words.

5. 1580
6. 3402
7. 7090
8. 6129
9. 2005
10. 8900
11. 4037
12. 9748

Give the value of the underlined digit.

13. 5<u>4</u>13
14. 37<u>6</u>2
15. <u>2</u>924
16. 653<u>9</u>
17. 13<u>8</u>7
18. <u>6</u>850
19. 419<u>6</u>
20. 7<u>2</u>81

Which number is larger?

21. 4259 or 4295
22. 1608 or 1086
23. 3726 or 3627
24. 8407 or 8740

Which number is smaller?

25. 5193 or 5139
26. 2072 or 2207
27. 9518 or 8915
28. 6347 or 6437

Write these numbers in order, starting with the smallest.

29. 7896   7968   7869   7986
30. 5425   4552   5452   4525
31. 2120   2012   2102   2021
32. 2313   2133   3121   2311

What number do you reach?

33. Start at 26.
    Count on five 3s.

34. Start at 39.
    Count on eight 2s.

35. Start at 127.
    Count on four 6s.

36. Start at 85.
    Count on three 9s.

37. Start at 2900.
    Count on five 25s.

38. Start at 3864.
    Count on four 100s.

39. Start at 1370.
    Count on six 50s.

40. Start at 29.
    Count on seven 1000s.

Work out

41. 3626 + 10
42. 9594 + 10
43. 4861 − 10
44. 2307 − 10
45. 7483 + 100
46. 1958 + 100
47. 8275 − 100
48. 6019 − 100

Round each number to the nearest:

a) 10
b) 100
c) 1000.

49. 4937
50. 9752
51. 5429
52. 1875
53. 5284
54. 1056
55. 4628
56. 9361

What number do you reach?

57. Count back 4 from 0.
58. Count back 6 from 3.
59. Count back 7 from 1.
60. Count back 9 from 2.

61. Write the number shown by each letter.

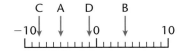

Write as Arabic numbers.

62. XIII
63. XLVIII
64. LXXXVI
65. XXV
66. LXII
67. XXXVII
68. XCIV
69. LXXIX

Write as Roman numerals.

70. 34
71. 18
72. 65
73. 29
74. 82
75. 56
76. 43
77. 97

Work out

1 70 + 80

2 900 + 400

3 160 − 70

4 1100 − 300

5 1734 + 400

6 2615 + 90

7 100 − 63

8 1000 − 150

9 85 + 69

10 98 + 32

11 107 − 59

12 124 − 67

Copy and complete.

13 80 + ☐ = 120

14 600 + ☐ = 700

15 140 − ☐ = 80

16 1500 − ☐ = 600

17 ☐ − 60 = 3187

18 ☐ + 85 = 5085

19 46 + ☐ = 100

20 750 + ☐ = 1000

21 53 + ☐ = 121

22 77 + ☐ = 173

23 ☐ − 75 = 67

24 ☐ − 86 = 29

Work out

25 4635 + 2678

26 3497 + 1805

27 3564 + 2497

28 5978 + 1683

29 6290 − 1875

30 4573 − 3926

31 7415 − 2538

32 9362 − 5845

Set out correctly and work out.

33 2846 + 967

34 4783 + 3269

35 3081 − 1427

36 8154 − 7273

Work out

37 8 × 6

38 12 × 4

39 7 × 9

40 9 × 3

41 6 × 1

42 5 × 12

43 24 ÷ 3

44 72 ÷ 6

45 28 ÷ 7

46 96 ÷ 12

47 50 ÷ 2

48 77 ÷ 11

49 60 × 2

50 80 × 70

51 900 × 8

52 500 × 0

53 4 × 110

54 70 × 50

55 4500 ÷ 9

56 1080 ÷ 12

57 4200 ÷ 6

58 400 ÷ 5

59 480 ÷ 8

60 3200 ÷ 4

Copy and complete.

61 ☐ × 5 = 30

62 ☐ × 9 = 72

63 ☐ × 4 = 240

64 ☐ × 11 = 1320

65 ☐ ÷ 6 = 9

66 ☐ ÷ 8 = 11

67 ☐ ÷ 12 = 30

68 ☐ ÷ 7 = 1200

Find all the factor pairs of:

69 12

70 55

71 28

72 40

73 17

74 36

75 45

76 84

Work out

77 638 × 6

78 857 × 5

79 249 × 8

80 690 × 9

Work out.

81 8)280

82 6)444

83 9)252

84 7)651

Set out correctly and work out.

85 679 × 4

86 438 × 9

87 765 × 7

88 586 × 8

89 570 ÷ 6

90 228 ÷ 3

91 196 ÷ 7

92 513 ÷ 9

Copy and complete the equivalent fractions.

1 $\frac{1}{3} = \frac{\square}{6}$

2 $\frac{1}{2} = \frac{\square}{8}$

3 $\frac{\square}{5} = \frac{4}{10}$

4 $\frac{\square}{6} = \frac{2}{12}$

5 $\frac{1}{4} = \frac{\square}{8}$

6 $\frac{2}{3} = \frac{\square}{12}$

7 $\frac{\square}{3} = \frac{4}{6}$

8 $\frac{\square}{6} = \frac{10}{12}$

9 $\frac{3}{4} = \frac{\square}{12}$

10 $\frac{4}{5} = \frac{\square}{10}$

11 $\frac{\square}{3} = \frac{6}{9}$

12 $\frac{\square}{3} = \frac{4}{12}$

Work out.

13 $\frac{3}{5} + \frac{1}{5}$

14 $\frac{4}{9} + \frac{4}{9}$

15 $\frac{7}{12} + \frac{1}{12}$

16 $\frac{2}{6} + \frac{3}{6}$

17 $\frac{5}{10} + \frac{2}{10}$

18 $\frac{3}{7} + \frac{4}{7}$

19 $\frac{8}{11} - \frac{2}{11}$

20 $\frac{5}{8} - \frac{3}{8}$

21 $1 - \frac{1}{3}$

22 $\frac{4}{6} - \frac{1}{6}$

23 $\frac{11}{12} - \frac{5}{12}$

24 $1 - \frac{7}{10}$

Find

25 $\frac{1}{5}$ of 60

26 $\frac{3}{4}$ of 28

27 $\frac{2}{3}$ of 12 litres

28 $\frac{7}{8}$ of 16 cm

29 $\frac{1}{12}$ of £132

30 $\frac{5}{6}$ of 30p

31 $\frac{3}{10}$ of 500 g

32 $\frac{7}{10}$ of 800 ml

33 $\frac{1}{10}$ of £3600

34 $\frac{5}{100}$ of 4000 kg

35 $\frac{9}{10}$ of 290 km

36 $\frac{4}{100}$ of 1200 m

What number do you reach?

37 Start at $\frac{3}{10}$. Count on 4 steps of $\frac{1}{10}$.

38 Start at $\frac{7}{8}$. Count back 5 steps of $\frac{1}{8}$.

39 Start at $\frac{5}{12}$. Count on 6 steps of $\frac{1}{12}$.

40 Start at 1. Count back 4 steps of $\frac{1}{9}$.

Write as decimals.

41 $\frac{3}{10}$

42 $\frac{72}{100}$

43 $\frac{1}{4}$

44 $\frac{6}{10}$

45 $\frac{19}{100}$

46 $\frac{1}{2}$

47 $\frac{48}{100}$

48 $\frac{9}{10}$

49 $\frac{53}{100}$

50 $\frac{3}{4}$

51 $\frac{2}{10}$

52 $\frac{86}{100}$

Divide each number by:

a) 10   **b)** 100.

53 45

54 10

55 4

56 28

57 99

58 2

59 30

60 83

61 6

62 57

63 80

64 5

Give the value of the underlined figure in each of these numbers.

65 5·7<u>3</u>

66 60·<u>2</u>

67 <u>7</u>·49

68 12·6<u>2</u>

69 <u>3</u>·1

70 0·9<u>5</u>

71 <u>4</u>28·3

72 <u>3</u>4·51

73 6·0<u>8</u>

74 1<u>9</u>·7

75 0·<u>5</u>4

76 97·8<u>6</u>

Arrange in order, smallest first.

77 5·11, 1·15, 1·05, 5·5, 1·5

78 0·9, 2·9, 0·92, 0·29, 2·29

79 8·33, 3·08, 8·3, 3·8, 3·38

80 4·6, 6·46, 40·6, 6·6, 4·46

Round to the nearest whole one.

81 4·7

82 37·5

83 6·1

84 42·3

85 1·9

86 85·6

87 19·2

88 3·8

89 28·4

90 70·5

91 2·7

92 61·1

Copy and complete.

1 85 mm = ☐ cm

2 4·1 cm = ☐ mm

3 26 cm = ☐ m

4 993 cm = ☐ m

5 0·45 m = ☐ cm

6 7·2 m = ☐ cm

7 5300 m = ☐ km

8 1·42 km = ☐ m

9 3800 g = ☐ kg

10 8260 g = ☐ kg

11 2·9 kg = ☐ g

12 0·74 kg = ☐ g

13 4500 ml = ☐ litres

14 1670 ml = ☐ litres

15 9·1 litres = ☐ ml

16 6·59 litres = ☐ ml

17 180 seconds = ☐ mins

18 5 minutes = ☐ secs.

19 10 hours = ☐ mins

20 90 minutes = ☐ hours

21 24 months = ☐ years

22 50 years = ☐ months

23 21 days = ☐ weeks

24 20 weeks = ☐ days

Measure the sides of each shape and work out the perimeters.

25

26
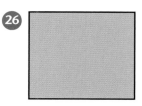

For each of the following shapes work out:

a) the perimeter

b) the area.

27 rectangle
sides 11 cm, 5 cm

28 square
sides 12 cm

29 rectangle
sides 20 m, 9 m

For each shape work out:

a) the missing lengths x and y

b) the perimeter
(all lengths are in cm.)

30
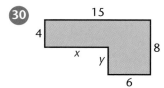

31
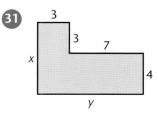

32 Copy and complete the table showing equivalent 12-hour and 24-hour clock times.

12-hour	24-hour
8:46 am	08:46
3:17 pm	
9:53 am	
10:09 pm	
1:26 am	
	11:41
	19:34
	14:02
	06:58
	23:16

33 Wilma pays £5 for her shopping. She receives £1·63 change. How much has she spent?

34 Wilbur earns £85 a day. How much does he earn in eight days?

35 Twelve eggs cost £3. What does one cost?

36 A quarter of a kilogram of brown flour is mixed with 375 g of white flour. What is the total weight of the mixture?

37 A jug holds 800 ml of drink. It is poured equally into five glasses. How much drink is in each glass?

38 Eight 30 cm strips are cut from a 5 m roll of tape. How much is left?

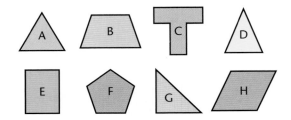

1 Which of the above shapes:

a) are quadrilaterals

b) are triangles

c) have all sides equal

d) have one or more pairs of perpendicular sides

e) have one or more pairs of parallel sides

f) have one or more obtuse angles

g) have no line of symmetry

h) have more than one line of symmetry?

2 Copy the symmetrical shapes. Draw on all the lines of symmetry.

3 Write each group of angles in order of size, smallest first.

Place the angles in each shape in order of size, smallest first.

4 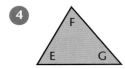 **5**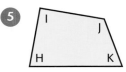

6 Decide if each of the above angles A–K is:

a) a right angle

b) acute

c) obtuse.

Draw and label the following:

7 TRIANGLES
isosceles
scalene
right-angled
equilateral

8 QUADRILATERALS
rhombus
trapezium
parallelogram
kite

9 Give the co-ordinates of these letters.

C F
K W
L J
H X

10 Which letter is at:

a) (2, 2) c) (1, 5) e) (0, 3)

b) (5, 0) d) (3, 4) f) (4, 1)

11 Start at the co-ordinate given. Follow the direction. Write down the letter you find.

a) (2, 4) Right 3 Down 2

b) (4, 1) Left 4 Up 3

c) (2, 0) Right 2 Up 5

d) (3, 5) Left 3 Down 4

Copy the above grid. Join up each set of points in the given order to form a shape. Label each shape.

12 (4, 0)(3, 2)(5, 3)(4, 0)

13 (1, 2)(0, 3)(2, 5)(3, 4)(1, 2)

14 Use squared paper. Copy each shape and the mirror line and draw the reflection.

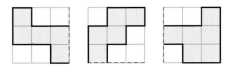

TEST 1

1. What is 500 more than 9528?

2. Write 0·18 as a fraction.

3. A one litre bottle of milk has 350 ml left. How much has been used?

4. What is 12 nines?

5. Count back 7 from 2. What number do you reach?

6. How many 6 cm lengths can be cut from 48 cm of string?

7. Subtract 80 from 5720.

8. A rectangle is 9 cm long and has an area of 63 cm². What is its width?

9. Round 2406 to the nearest ten.

10. Add 65 and 77.

11. How many days make six weeks?

12. Take five eighths from one.

13. What needs to be added to change 1083 to 1103?

14. What is the twentieth multiple of three?

15. A bag of sweets costs 79p. Jason pays £2. How much change is he given?

16. What is the value of the 5 in 47·52?

17. What number do you reach if you count on 6 fours from 15?

18. Write 87 as Roman numerals.

19. Train tickets cost £8 each. How many can be bought for £56?

20. What is 4·9 kg in grams?

21. Find the difference between 4630 and 4030.

22. How many years is 60 months?

23. Safa gets on the bus at 7:42. She gets off 25 minutes later. At what time does she get off the bus?

24. Multiply 2·97 by 10.

TEST 2

1. Divide 81 by 9.

2. What number is 200 times greater than 8?

3. Gayle spends £79 in one shop and £32 in another. How much has she spent altogether?

4. Write five thousand and ninety-four in figures.

5. Write seven hundredths as a decimal fraction.

6. What is 35 divided by 7?

7. What would the temperature be if it was 4°C and fell 6°?

8. Write 3160 m as kilometres.

9. Find the difference between 10 000 and 2500.

10. What is the area of a rectangle 9 cm long and 4 cm wide?

11. Write LXIV as Arabic numbers.

12. What needs to be added to three tenths to make nine tenths?

13. How many 20p coins make £10?

14. Take 48 from 120.

15. Write 9:52 pm in 24-hour clock time.

16. What is 100 less than 3047?

17. What is the sum of 58 and 65?

18. Find the perimeter of a triangle with three equal sides each 1·2 m long.

19. A book costs £3·70. Robbie buys it for half price. What does he pay?

20. Divide 8 by 100.

21. Round 8258 to the nearest hundred.

22. How many elevens make 132?

23. Pens cost 45p each. How much change would you receive if you bought ten pens and paid with a 10 pound note?

24. What is 620 less than 3942?

How to learn a times table.

BY YOURSELF

1. Read the table over and over.
2. Cover the table and say it out loud or in your mind.
3. Say it more and more quickly.
4. Try to say the table backwards.

WITH A FRIEND

Ask each other questions like:

What is 9 times 6?

Multiply 7 by 11.

How many eights make 72?

Divide 60 by 12.

✗	1	2	3	4	5	6	7	8	9	10	11	12
ONES	1	2	3	4	5	6	7	8	9	10	11	12
TWOS	2	4	6	8	10	12	14	16	18	20	22	24
THREES	3	6	9	12	15	18	21	24	27	30	33	36
FOURS	4	8	12	16	20	24	28	32	36	40	44	48
FIVES	5	10	15	20	25	30	35	40	45	50	55	60
SIXES	6	12	18	24	30	36	42	48	54	60	66	72
SEVENS	7	14	21	28	35	42	49	56	63	70	77	84
EIGHTS	8	16	24	32	40	48	56	64	72	80	88	96
NINES	9	18	27	36	45	54	63	72	81	90	99	108
TENS	10	20	30	40	50	60	70	80	90	100	110	120
ELEVENS	11	22	33	44	55	66	77	88	99	110	121	132
TWELVES	12	24	36	48	60	72	84	96	108	120	132	144